ROOTS
OF
REFORM:
CHALLENGING THE ASSUMPTIONS
THAT CONTROL EDUCATION REFORM

by
Terry A. Astuto
New York University

David L. Clark
University of North Carolina at Chapel Hill

Anne-Marie Read
~sity of North Carolina at Chapel Hill

Kathleen McGree
¡versity of Virginia

Pelton Fernandez
· of Virginia

ᶠrom the
ᐟ Improvement

Pᵣ.

Cover design by Victoria Voelker

Library of Congress Catalog Number 94-65000
ISBN 0-87367-464-2
Copyright © 1994 by the Phi Delta Kappa Educational Foundation
Bloomington, Indiana

ACKNOWLEDGMENTS

The authors wish to acknowledge the support of the Regional Laboratory for Educational Improvement of the Northeast and Islands during the development of this book. The Laboratory's Executive Director, David Crandall, provided criticism of the manuscript; and the first three sections of the document were discussed by many members of the Laboratory staff. We appreciate the intensive reviews of the manuscript provided by Professor Richard F. Elmore, Harvard University; Professor Michelle Fine, City University of New York Graduate Center; Professor Henry Giroux, Pennsylvania State University; and Professor George Noblit, University of North Carolina at Chapel Hill. The range, diversity, and depth of their analyses of the first five sections of the book improved the quality of the work measurably — even in cases where we ultimately failed to implement their suggestions.

TABLE OF CONTENTS

INTRODUCTION

The Education reform movement that began in the 1980s has produced disappointing and unsatisfactory results. Policy makers who have labored over federal, state, and local reform initiatives blame the failure on the reluctance or incompetence of practitioners. Educators working at the school and classroom levels blame policy makers for their lack of understanding of the real life of the school. Many of the parties involved blame the victims or, more accurately, they would blame the victims had they not been instructed about the political inappropriateness of doing so. In this case, the victims are not only students who are unprepared to cope with conventional school regulations, procedures, and requirements, but also the families and parents of these children and youth. Everyone wants to blame the delivery systems that fragment the social, medical, psychological, nutritional, and educational resources and services for children.

Whoever or whatever is to blame for the failure, many currently popular reforms could be dismissed as impractical, even ridiculous, if they were not being devised and supported by apparently credible and powerful advocates — and if the consequences of their failure were not so devastating to a generation of American youth. Education reform in the United States must not fail. City school systems cannot be dismissed as unworkable. Youngsters from low-income households can not be consigned to poverty-ridden schools.

This book is not despairing. We believe the reform movement needs to be reformulated. We also believe that the reformation is possible and even likely, if the current failure of reform can be better understood and used as the basis for a new and vigorous effort to save our children and our schools.

The basic causes of the failure, we will argue, are the narrow limits of imagination that have governed the reform proposals. For example, the establishment by states of minimum testing standards, with sanctions for districts not meeting the standards, is essentially a paper transaction that may threaten a handful of underproducing districts. Not surprisingly, those districts almost always include high concentrations of poverty. For such districts, a proposal to convert their schools into youth service centers that would be open 24 hours a day, 365 days a year, serving three healthy meals to their students, and providing social, psychological, and medical services would be an authentic proposal for reform. Instead, they are counseled to adopt an outcomes-based education program that is in alignment with the standardized test being used to assess their effectiveness.

Why focus on implementing a site-based management system for high schools while retaining a 45- to 50-minute daily schedule of six to eight class periods that ensures that most high school teachers will never get to know anything about the lives of the 150 to 200 students that pass by them each day? Does anyone believe that such an education structure provides the time for English teachers to tutor their students in writing, or that it provides adult role models for those youngsters who have few such models in their home or community setting, or that it provides an opportunity for individualized instruction and counseling for students? Should we believe that schools are so different from other organizations that testing "rejects" is an effective system for increasing the quality of the organization's core processes?

What sort of reform is this anyway? In our opinion it is a reform movement rooted in a nested set of assumptions that constrains the proposition, let alone the implementation, of changes required in our schools. For the past 24 months we have been about the task of attempting to identify the assumptions employed by policy makers, education researchers, administrators, and classroom practitioners that influence, in some cases govern, the reform proposals that they consider practical or feasible. Our hunch was that many of these assumptions should not go unchallenged and that the aphoristic standing that they had been granted in devising education reforms was unwarranted.

Since our own backgrounds are in organizational theory, we were influenced by two landmark efforts undertaken in the field of organizational studies 30 to 35 years ago. In the mid-1950s, Chris Argyris surveyed the existing research literature on human behavior. His intent was to compare these findings with the existing knowledge base in organizational studies and organizational practice. The result, published in 1957 under the title *Personality and Organization*, allowed students and practitioners of administration to examine the "lack of congruency between the needs of healthy individuals and the demands of the formal organization" (p. 233). Argyris posited a set of credible counter-assumptions about human development needs that provided a rationale for managers to undertake reforms that were more than simply cosmetic alterations of earlier managerial practice.

In 1960, Douglas McGregor published *The Human Side of Enterprise*, in which he argued:

> The theoretical assumptions management holds about controlling its human resources determines the whole character of the

2

enterprise. . . . The key question of top management is: What are your assumptions (implicit as well as explicit) about the most effective way to manage people? (p. x)

McGregor juxtaposed the assumptions held by most employers about their employees against a set of generalizations that he argued were derived from "the accumulation of knowledge about human behavior in many specialized fields" (p. 47).

The impact of the work completed by Argyris, McGregor, and their colleagues in the late 1950s and 1960s (e.g., Bennis, Drucker, Gouldner, Likert, and Presthus) was intended less to establish a new orthodoxy than to remove aphoristic status from the conventional wisdom of the field. By positing and justifying counter-propositions that were supported by either the knowledge base of human behavior and organizational studies or by exceptional managerial policy and practice, they were able to stimulate new ways of thinking about the structure of organizations and the people in them.

Our work over the past 24 months is indebted to these pioneers in organizational theory. We examined the recent literature of research, policy, and practice about:

- the political context of education,
- the social context of education,
- the organizational structure of schools,
- the people in educational organizations, and
- the organizational and educational processes in schools.

First, we considered each of these fields of literature individually. Our search was for the major assumptions that policy makers, practitioners, and scholars might hold (implicitly or explicitly) about the best way to operate schools and to educate children. We recorded conventional, neo-orthodox, and nonorthodox theoretical positions, data-based research findings, and reports of ordinary and exceptional practice. Whenever we discovered dominant, conventional views, we searched for counterpoints to challenge the assumptions underlying those views. If the counterpoints were justified by research, successful practice, or persuasive logic, we noted them.

Second, not by our original design but by serendipity, we noted that the assumptions were nested across the domains of inquiry. This linkage of individually powerful assumptions suggested to us that our original concern about the extent to which a set of dominant assumptions was constraining education reform probably was justified.

3

Throughout this short volume, readers will note an assumption held by the authors that we should make explicit. Our primary concern about the efficacy of the American school system is focused on the least-served population in the schools: children of poverty. This is our focus because we have become convinced that the center of the country's education crisis rests with these students.

Overwhelmingly, by number, the children of poverty are the students who drop out of school, become in-school dropouts, are segregated as "at-risk" and underachieving, confront repeated failures academically and socially, and are exposed to the dangers of criminal subcultures in their non-school lives. Schools must take on a richer, more significant mission for these youngsters. Their lives demand a commitment of social responsibility that currently is missing in child and family policy in the United States. This group also is the fastest-growing population of public school children in the United States. Failure to respond to their needs will wreak havoc in the public schools and in American society as a whole.

Fortunately, as we will attempt to demonstrate, the reforms needed to respond to this population are very likely to have efficacious results for all children and youth and to raise the quality of American public schools across the board.

We are not oblivious to other limitations in American public schools. Schools for the 21st century demand striking changes for all students — changes that should be based on a new vision of learning that will allow students to participate effectively and creatively in a post-modern world. That vision will not be generated by attending to surrogate purposes for American schools. We must not legitimize our interest in serving the young on grounds of preparing them to fit the needs of our business and industrial complex, nor to meet the demands of international economic competition, nor to reduce subsequent costs of incarceration, health care, or social ills. The vision will come from focusing on the needs of children and youth, not the needs of others in society. If we can do that, society will be well-served by a new generation of thoughtful, critical, creative leaders.

In the pages that follow, we have attempted to present a small set of controlling assumptions from each of the five domains of study. Each controlling assumption is examined in relation to a counter-assumption. We do not claim aphoristic standing for either postulation. The intent of this study is to broaden rather than narrow the dialogue surrounding education reform. Our imagination is insufficient to picture the most effective future of education reform. However, the evidence we discovered convinced us that more of the same will not be adequate to the task confronting us. What we have experienced so far are practices and policies rooted firmly in a set of dominant assumptions that reflect orthodox views and conservative interpretations of the knowledge bases and practices of organizational studies, schooling, and education policy.

CHAPTER ONE

ASSUMPTIONS ABOUT THE POLITICAL CONTEXT OF SCHOOLING

The power of dominant assumptions to influence education reform proposals and initiatives was made strikingly clear with the election in 1980 of a conservative President who exhibited a strong interest in education. By the end of Ronald Reagan's first 12 months in office, the lexicon of terms that controlled the discussion of education policy had changed drastically from equity to excellence, standards of performance, and individual competition; from needs and access to ability, selectivity, and minimum entrance standards; from social and welfare concerns to economic and productivity concerns; from the common school to parental choice and privatization; from federal interests and initiatives to state and local interests and initiatives (Clark and Astuto 1989*a*).

By 1992, the latter lexicon of terms had been reified and enacted in a set of reforms that were advocated or adopted at national, state, and local levels. Performance standards for individuals and school systems have been established and used as the sole or primary basis for comparisons of educational productivity. Test specialists and evaluators are grappling with the feasibility of "authentic" testing and the development of an acceptable national test for use in elementary and secondary schools. Education has been linked closely to business and industry, and the success of schools in preparing graduates for employment is posited as the keystone outcome of schooling.

In the administrations of both Presidents Reagan and Bush, funds were sought from Congress to support privatization of schooling; and several states adopted voucher plans to facilitate parental choice of private schools. Three of the four most popular public school innovations of the 1990s clearly reflect the new education policy orthodoxy: out-

7

comes-based education, total quality management, and state and national objective testing programs to measure education quality.

The unexpectedly swift change in political policy preferences in education might be explained as simply the mercurial nature of policy choices when a middle-of-the-road liberal administration is replaced by an avowedly conservative one. We believe there is more to it than that.

Public opinion polls on education for two decades preceding the presidential election of 1980 indicated at least a half-hearted support by the American public of the more liberal education agenda of that period. The broad-based liberal initiative of the 1960s was the Elementary and Secondary Education Act of 1965 (ESEA). Then the initiatives of the 1970s focused on equity in schooling for women and the handicapped.

We are not concerned with the particular policy preferences that are chosen in different eras. Our concern is that political preferences that dominate the public mind for extended time periods begin to assume aphoristic status. Unchallenged, they narrow the imagination and obscure the negative trade-offs inherent in any policy choice. We will frame this concern in the discussion that follows by examining three contemporary political emphases in education: 1) the purposes of schooling, 2) the conditions that stimulate organizational and individual achievement in schools, and 3) the external resources and control mechanisms needed for effective reform.

Purposes of Schooling

Much of the current debate about reform in education boils down to the question of whether one assumes that schools are capable of interrupting the relationship between socioeconomic status and educational achievement. Despite the shibboleth that all children can learn, the fact is that a variety of school practices suggest that the perception of what they can learn, how much they can learn, and to what end their learning can be put in the real world is conjectural.

Meritocracy and Universality

In fact there are two quite different assumptions about the basic purpose of education for children and youth and for the productive capacity of the country. These assumptions may be framed as:

> The purpose of schooling in a democracy is to allow children and youth to progress and develop on the basis of their own ability and talent, that is, meritocratically.

8

OR

> The purpose of schooling in a democracy is to extend the
> benefits of the society to all children and youth by preparing
> them to access those benefits.

The impact of a meritocratic education system is to exclude large segments of the student population from the societal fruits and rewards of meritocracy. The crisis in American schools is inseparable from the crisis in American society.

Poor children — predominantly children of color — are dying, literally and figuratively, at a young age. Poverty in America is now inversely related to age. Children aged birth to six are more likely to live in poor households than any other age group in our society. Larger and larger groups of children are entering school unprepared to face the challenges of learning that will be presented to them. Although it is true that many social services could and should be extended to these youngsters to offset the unhealthy effects of poverty, it is also true that American schools, on their own, could be reformed to provide support that would significantly enhance the opportunities for successful learning by these youngsters. If the mission of the school were to include all children in the sunlight of this society, no excuse would suffice to justify or explain away the school's failure to guarantee successful education for each child.

This point was captured by Ronald Edmonds when he was leading a school reform effort that became designated as the Instructionally Effective Schools (IES) movement:

> How many effective schools would you have to see to be persuaded of the educability of poor children? If your answer is more than one, then I submit that you have reasons of your own for preferring to believe that basic pupil performance derives from family background instead of school response to family background. (Edmonds 1979, p. 16)

One of these reasons might be the assumption that the purpose of schooling is meritocratic rather than universalistic. Without denying the attractiveness of certain theoretical features of meritocracy and the common school, Angus (1989) argued:

> Any number of scholars working within various conflict perspectives have demonstrated that apparently neutral school practices which have usually been regarded as fair, open, and meritocratic contribute to the reproduction of existing social and economic arrangements. (p. 80)

The acceptability of meritocracy depends on a level field of potential performance by all participants. Without this condition, meritocracy results in the use of education practices that exclude disadvantaged students from any opportunity for a successful education in the public schools.

Instrumentality and Entitlement

A second policy issue surrounding the purpose of schooling is the raison d'être for public involvement in education. During the 1980s, the issue surfaced in bald economic terms. American schools were said to be failing to prepare students for the world of work and were contributing to the increasing lack of competitiveness of the United States in the world market. There is a contrasting view that places the well-being or advantage of the student at the heart of the matter. These two positions often are referred to as instrumentality and entitlement:

> The test of the efficacy of an education system is its instrumental contribution to the goals of society.

> ### OR

> The test of the efficacy of an education system is the extent to which it meets the entitlement of all children to access the benefits of their society.

The temptation is to assert that these positions are not in conflict, that they both can be met by an enlightened democratic society. Perhaps so, but only if the position of entitlement is pre-established. And the accomplishment of that end not only is far from realized in the United States, but will require a massive infusion of resources to achieve. Valerie Polakow (1992) noted that the state of deprivation confronted by America's poor children has reached a point at which the language of early education and intervention must become "a language of existential entitlement" rather than a language of "instrumentalism" (p. 303).

Polakow cited recent census data from the Children's Defense Fund, documenting 13.4 million children living in poverty, 9.8 million children lacking health insurance, and 100,000 children homeless on any given night (p. 296). Stunning data support the crisis of poverty beyond early childhood through adolescence. Over half of all school-age children in Detroit, for example, were living in poverty in 1992 — a dismal "first" for one of the country's major cities.

10

However, dramatic data on childhood poverty should not be required to justify the argument for entitlement in a democratic society nor to justify the argument against inadequate outcomes for students. More to the point is Jonathan Kozol's (1992) plaint that "students are described, and valued, not as children but as 'workers'. They are seen as future 'assets' or 'productive units'. . . but not as human beings who have value in themselves" (p. 277). Every student is living the only life he or she will ever experience; and if the school, by intent, neglect, or oversight, makes that life less than it could be, a crime has been committed in and by a cherished public institution.

None of this argument is to discount the data that can be mustered in an instrumental justification for an enlightened policy toward education reform. Data that assert the economic wisdom of avoiding problems of crime, drugs, violence, and incarceration are technically compelling and, in a sense, benign. Arguments that focus on preparation for the world of work or that explore the theme that the failure of the education system is a crisis because it endangers the economic health of the country may have less benign consequences. For example, such arguments may lead schools to tracking students toward employment based on socioeconomic status. In either instance, we concur with Edgar Friedenberg's (1991) comment on the Charles Kuralt-Roger Mudd approach to the education crisis as seen in their television documentaries for CBS and PBS:

> I am . . . grossed out by the argument that poor children should be given improved medical care and adequate food so that they will do better in school and become more economically productive. . . . The views on education of Americans who can find no more compelling reason than this for caring for their sick or starving children can be of very little interest. (p. 15)

This is the heart of the matter. The student's entitlement to life, liberty, and the pursuit of happiness is a pre-ordinal condition of existence that should make instrumentalism superfluous in a democratic society. That it does not is a commentary on the ill-health of our society. That instrumentalism should preempt entitlement opens the possibility that the purpose of education can be distorted from fulfilling the needs of youth to securing a profit to society.

Conditions to Stimulate Achievement

While everyone is concerned with increasing student performance in school, there are quite different assumptions made about the relative responsibility of the student and the school in the process.

Individual Responsibility and Institutional Responsiveness

Persons who accept a meritocratic view of schooling obviously believe that the bulk of the responsibility lies with the student. Those who argue a universalistic view see administrators, teachers, and the capacity of the school to respond to diverse learners as central variables in achievement. These positions can be characterized as follows:

> Achievement in school rests predominantly in the hands of the individual student.

> ### OR

> Individual achievement in school is influenced markedly by the adjustment of the school to the student client.

No one doubts that some youngsters who seem to have everything going against them succeed in school, or that others who are privileged by all material advantages are dropouts. The issue is not whether there are outliers who prove the exception to the rule, but rather what the rule is. Many who doubt the educability of poor children believe that people get what they work for and deserve. The dramatic success stories of penniless immigrants rising to affluence and power by dint of effort and talent form a charming but misleading myth of American society. The best predictor of the ultimate socioeconomic status of a child in this country is, and has been historically, the socioeconomic status of the child's family. Most immigrant families live in poverty for generations. Ours is not a classless society. Individual effort and talent are thwarted by family and institutional circumstances well before birth and throughout life.

The disadvantages of poverty cannot be overcome by concentrating on preschool or early childhood intervention programs. In a society where larger numbers and percentages of children are living in poor households each year, schools must provide support systems for large numbers of students throughout their school years. The traditional American view that early intervention is all that most persons need to overcome poverty is belied by the evidence of previous child and family support programs. The cycle of poverty is a negative, amplifying cycle that has to be broken by consistent and persistent efforts to adjust public service agencies to the needs of their clients. Only then might the truism that individual achievement rests in the hands of the student turn out to be true.

The good news is that some of the public schools in this society do contravene the predetermined system of individual progress by class and race. Many more could if they were designed to do so. Schools, for example, could become nurturing, caring, learning environments designed to attack debilitating factors associated with poverty, such as neglect, abuse, hunger, disease, deprivation of learning stimuli, and absence of adult role models. The primary criterion for determining the allocation of school resources could become nurturing the talents of each student. The mindset of the school's professional staff could be to prevent failure by any child. The structure of schooling and the relationship of professional staff to students could be adjusted to fit the needs of the school's clients. That this not only could but should be the case is a simple extension of the assumption of entitlement presented in the preceding section.

Competition and Standards, Cooperation and Support

In addition to the locus of responsibility for achievement, policy makers and others concerned with school reform differ in their assumptions about the role of standards, competition, and comparative systems of assessment as stimulators of high achievement. In the past decade, the conflicting views of policy makers and practitioners have been as follows:

> Educational achievement is enhanced by high standards, competition, and comparative assessment of students, schools, and school districts.

> **OR**

> Educational achievement is enhanced by conditions of cooperation that reflect trust, confidence, support, and challenge among and between teachers and learners.

One of the metaphors used to think about schooling is "the game," but not just any game. Amusement, recreation, or play are not what most people have in mind. Rather, "the game" is about winning and losing. An education reform movement rooted in standards, testing, and selectivity is a movement that embraces competition as the driving force behind institutional productivity. In the minds of many reformers, the American free-enterprise system is the model for the next generation of American schools. School survival will be decided by consumers in a high-stakes game for schools, teachers, and students. It is

13

noteworthy that the term "high stakes" is now commonplace among testing specialists and education policy makers.

A stark example of reformers' confidence in grading and standards recently was offered by Clifford Adelman, Director of the Division of Higher Education in the Office of Educational Research and Improvement, U.S. Department of Education. Adelman (1993) contended that the failure to "judge. . . the quality of individual performance" by students hides information from potential employers and provides "distorted conceptions of their own achievement" to students. He asserted:

> The inclusion of information concerning student performance on diplomas and degrees would help restore our educational credentials as valid currency. Posting these judgments would open doors for our children. If they pursue a higher level of education, we and they and their eventual employers will know the true nature of their achievement. (p. 21)

The unspoken assumption in the Adelman article is that students will strive for and achieve higher performance under such conditions. A similar view of the efficacy of competition and comparative assessment leads states to rank school districts and schools by the average achievement of their students.

There is an alternative view of education that sees schools as communities of learners, young and old, committed to supporting one another in the quest to fulfill their human potential. The accumulated evidence on successful schools and student achievement strongly suggests that competitive environments shatter the conditions of trust, caring, and cooperation that are most conducive to learning, innovation, and creativity and that those environments have the most negative consequences for those learners least able to compete successfully. Positive reinforcement and attainable challenges, requisites for learning, are nearly impossible to sustain in an environment of winners and losers. If professionals are judged on the basis of standardized tests, they will emphasize in their instruction the learning needed to pass those tests. If students are judged by such tests, those unable to meet those challenges will exhibit the symptoms of failure, such as resistance, withdrawal, and disruption. Extending the labeling and classifying of students into adulthood raises the stakes inherent in testing and places at further disadvantage those students who are ill-served by schools — poor children and those disadvantaged by racism and sexism.

The only real hope for reversing negative environmental influences on student learning rests in classrooms that exemplify cooperation, giving, and caring. The proof of such a system will be a narrowing of the gap between the haves and have-nots in our society.

External Resources and Control

Education reform movements are fueled by crises that typically are posed in political hyperbole: Sputnik and the space race in the late 1950s, the War on Poverty in the 1960s and early 1970s, *A Nation at Risk* in the 1980s. The difficulty with hyperbole-driven reform is that it spawns spurious assumptions that stick in the minds of reformers, practitioners, and the general public.

Stable and Increased Investments

One of the most troublesome current assumptions involves the relationship of expenditures for education to education reform. The counter assumption is a view of the relationship between expenditure and performance found in most organizational literature.

> Additional resource investments in public education will not increase system performance and are unnecessary to effect and sustain major reform in schools.

> **OR**

> Additional resource investments in public education will increase system performance and will affect the rate and scope of major reform in schools.

Three assumptions are made by those who advocate reform without added investment in education. First is the argument that the system already is richly funded in contrast to education systems in other industrialized countries. Second is the contention that the United States literally cannot afford higher taxes for social services. Third is the argument that effective organizations are "lean and mean," thus additional investment in education would be unlikely to result in higher productivity. In this last regard, President Reagan argued that a reverse relationship exists between investment and outcome in education. In other words, the President believed that the decline in school productivity prior to the 1980s was caused by federal investments in education during the 1960s and 1970s.

These are especially troublesome assumptions in relation to education reform, since a number of the options that immediately occur to reformers (for example, keeping schools open for 12 months a year or

24 hours a day, feeding children three meals a day, or increasing opportunities for students to have intensive contact with adult tutors) have substantial costs attached to them.

Ample evidence contests the assertion regarding the cost of American elementary and secondary education. Berliner (1992) reported:

> In 1988 dollars we rank ninth among 16 industrialized nations in per pupil expenditures in grades K-12, spending 14% less than Germany, 30% less than Japan, and 51% less than Switzerland. (p. 28)

Presidents Reagan and Bush resisted "throwing money at education" to solve its problems. They chose to view the American public school system as one with rich resources already invested in its performance, and these arguments frequently were tied directly to occasions for reform. For example, at the Education Summit in 1989, President Bush noted that the United States "lavishes unsurpassed resources on [our children's] schooling" (Berliner 1992, p. 29). This is simply not so. Organizational experts would be shocked if an organization spending 14% or 30% or 51% less than its competitor was able to maintain a competitive edge or even equity with that competitor.

The contention that the United States simply has no more funds to invest in education makes an aphorism out of a choice. Berliner (1992, p. 28) reported that 13 of 16 industrialized nations "spent a greater percent of per capita income on K-12 education" than the United States. This is not surprising, since we have chosen to invest less than many other nations in all child-welfare programs. The United States, ranking second in per capita income, does not rank in the top 10 on any significant indicator of child welfare. This record of choice in regard to tolerating child and family poverty is highlighted through international comparisons that document a consistent pattern of neglect:

- In the United States more than 21% of persons living in families with children are living in poverty. All European and Scandinavian countries have less than half that rate. In Norway and Sweden, the rate was 5.0% and 5.2%; in Germany, 2.8% (Coder, Rainwater, and Smeeding 1989, p. 323).
- "Infant mortality in the United States places it 20th in the world, behind such countries as Spain and Singapore . . . Ireland and Costa Rica" (Hewlett 1991, pp. 12, 35).
- "Almost all the Continental European countries [and Japan] finance free or low-fee optional preschool or child care for children from age three or younger up to school age" (Hamburg 1992,

16

p. 122). In the United States, children in families with incomes under $10,000 a year have only a one-in-six chance of being enrolled in a pre-primary school.

So much for an even field. The concern over the national debt and the unpopularity of taxation is placed in perspective by comparing the tax levels in the United States and other industrialized nations. American citizens may choose to resist additional taxation or choose to invest in programs other than education and child and family welfare, but the argument to do so is not aphoristic; it needs to be debated as an open question.

Last is the assertion that additional investments, if they were made, would not result in improved performance. The issue, if there is one, needs to be stated more narrowly: Which investments for which purposes? Some organizations have become wasteful and bloated, including some in education. But slack time and resources may be related positively to organizational outcomes. Clearly, highly innovative companies are funded at levels that allow for experimentation.

The common argument, posed by those who doubt the efficacy of investing in education, selects a "worst case" school district and asserts that money invested in that district would do no good under current conditions. Probably so. A bankrupt corporation is not simply provided with an open purse to pursue past practices. But neither should anyone expect that a bankrupt corporation will improve without relief from debt and funds to reorganize. Bankrupt school districts (financially or productively) should be treated in the same fashion.

The real issue is that most American public schools are not bankrupt but struggle with budgetary levels that constrain conditions for improvement. Many schools work with a pittance for staff development, little or nothing for research and development, sharply limited funds to reassign teachers for curriculum or materials development, allocations that force the acceptance of assembly-line schedules at the high school level, and class sizes that block the development of teacher-student work teams. And money is not being invested where the worst problems exist. As education advocates for the poor are demonstrating in state after state, funding systems for local schools are inherently unfair. They invariably favor wealthy districts and penalize poor districts.

In the final analysis, schools behave similarly to all organizations. The well-supported school districts and schools, in which resources meet or exceed demands, tend to succeed. Districts and schools deprived of adequate resources tend to fail. Where the resource shortfall is extreme and the demands for services are high, the failure can be dramatic.

Bankruptcy and Viability

The prior discussion of funding is not convincing to one group of critics that challenges the efficacy of American schools, advocates of open parental choice of schools through some form of voucher system to transfer public funds to private schools. However, the privatization of schooling is not a dominant assumption. The two contending positions can be framed as:

> The viability of the American public school system is so low that external agencies must design and control the needed reform.

OR

> The viability of American public schools is exhibited by current performance in relation to past performance and by international comparisons of student achievement.

The charge of pervasive ineffectiveness in American public schools was made by the report of the National Commission on Excellence in Education in *A Nation at Risk* (1983). This widely publicized and broadly distributed report charged the public schools hyperbolically with malfeasance akin to that of a foreign power that had set about the destruction of the United States. *A Nation at Risk* was followed by a series of other, more scholarly, commission reports that, in sum, portrayed the public schools not only as lagging seriously in international competition but as failing in critical areas to meet the needs of children and youth. The public policy debates ranged from abandoning the public schools in favor of privatization schemes to structuring reforms that emphasize performance monitoring through standardized testing and sanctions against failing school districts. This latter reform structure typically is administered at the state level and provides for state takeovers of under-performing districts.

More current evidence suggests that the diagnosis of the failure of the American public school system was both too general and too negative. All the available data need not be reviewed to suggest that the claim of ineffective performance by American schools is an exaggeration. There is no doubt that youngsters in school in 1980 and today were and are performing better than earlier generations. A recent report by the Strategic Studies Center of the Sandia National Laboratories indicated that:

- Performance on the National Assessment of Educational Progress (NAEP) has been steady or improving, with the greatest gains in basic skills.
- The reported decline in the Scholastic Aptitude Test (SAT) is due solely to the increase in the number of students in the bottom half of the class who are taking the test.
- One-fourth of today's students will obtain at least a bachelor's degree — the highest rate of attainment in the world.
- The overall technical degree attainment by the U.S. work force is the highest in the world (Huelskamp 1993, pp. 719-20).

More recent data on international comparisons that take into account similar sample populations indicate that American students do very well (Westbury 1992). However, no one challenges the existence of a crisis in American schools. Children of poverty are not succeeding in existing schools. Dropout rates are high. Disproportionate numbers of poor students are tracked into nonacademic programs and special education classes. Berliner (1992) offers a caustic summary of the effect of the misdirection of the reform effort away from a heightened consciousness of the failure of schools to meet the needs of the economically disadvantaged:

> The reforms they offer — higher standards, a tougher curriculum — with no increase in spending, will insure that the children of New Trier High School, near Chicago, and the children of Princeton, New Jersey, and the children of Manhasset, New York, will succeed even more than they do today. The children at P.S. 79 in the Bronx, New York, will fail at even greater rates than they do today. . . . Reforms of the kind being proposed will exacerbate the differences between the have and the have-not school districts. (pp. 55-56)

We agree with Berliner about the negative effects that heavy-handed state monitoring systems will have on the education of poor children. However, the long-range effect of relying on performance standards and testing to stimulate school reform will be to stultify a public school curriculum that is already too standardized and mechanistic for all children. Standards define culture, creating a uniform picture of national identity. The most prestigious standards are rooted in the disciplines but imposed on an interdisciplinary world.

The 21st century vision of American schools is not likely to arise from or be supported by political control of schools at the state level. Better clues to the future are provided by the reformers from within and outside the education profession (Boyer, Comer, Darling-Hammond, Goodlad, Lanier, Levin, Lieberman, Meier, Sizer) who offer alternative possibilities and then work with schools to realize those visions. No one imagines that external accountability for education at the state level is unimportant or unnecessary. But too many state policy makers believe only in tightening control through bureaucratic measures. This is nonsense. State legislatures, executive offices, and departments of public instruction are, as a rule, less effective bureaucracies than the districts and schools that they attempt to control.

Conclusion

The intent of this examination of alternative propositions about the political context of schooling in America has not been to introduce a new set of constraining counter-aphorisms into the ongoing debate over the reform of American education. The counter-propositions are presented and supported to broaden the range of viable choices. The current, dominant assumptions can and should be reduced from aphorisms to preferences. These preferences have given priority and advantage to one group of students in school at the expense of another — the affluent versus the poor. Therefore, the resolution of the conflict between the alternative preferences should be reached on the strength of competing evidence and a debate over values and the purposes of schooling.

The propositions are not simply independent assertions. Each interlocks with others to create a set of nearly inviolable constraints to debate. The beliefs are woven together into positions that have more to do with an overall political view of America's present and future than with a special interest in education. A meritocratic view of the education system excludes children and youth from the fruits of American society according to their economic level and ethnicity. But the view does not stand on its own. If individuals who hold this belief did not also hold the view that achievement in school rests in the will and effort of the students, one could imagine schools created to seek meritocratic ends for all students. However, such schools could not attain these ends without focusing major resources on the least-able learners. Such effort would require public school support at the level of the most effective meritocratic schools, the exclusive private academies that provide tutorial support for every student. Many of the least-supported students would need residential facilities for part or all of their schooling. All would require attention to health, nutrition, counseling, and dental care that is routine for the affluent segments of society.

The clustering of unexamined assumptions inhibits consideration of powerful reform alternatives. Some of the operating assumptions are simply factually wrong, such as the assumption regarding current levels of expenditure on schools in relation to competitor nations' spending. Some are debatable based on current evidence, such as the level of achievement on standardized tests by American school students versus students in other countries. Some reflect deep-seated political and human values, such as meritocracy versus universality. Others are trade-offs in which dual emphases might be achieved, such as competition versus cooperation.

If we are to avoid what Sarason (1990) labels the "predictable failure of educational reform," we must examine the assumptions of policy makers, reformers, and the public and initiate a debate that allows for the consideration of radical reform. Schools for the 21st century must not be envisioned as merely more efficient 20th century schools. They will be either radically different or essentially the same (Elmore 1990, pp. 289-97). The radical changes needed will violate some of the assumptions held by all, since our own assumptions, liberal or conservative, are derived from our experience with today's and yesterday's schools.

CHAPTER TWO

ASSUMPTIONS ABOUT THE SOCIAL CONTEXTS OF SCHOOLING

The power of the interactive relationship between schools and society was dramatized in the Coleman report (1966), which argued that variations in school achievement were accounted for predominantly by the socioeconomic status of students' families. The debates that followed the release of this national study moved consideration of the social context of education from the domains of sociology, school finance, and education philosophy to public discussions about the purposes of schooling, school expenditures and effectiveness, and eventually, issues of racism and sexism in American schooling. Despite the serious questions raised about the validity of the work of Coleman, the overall effect of the report was to stiffen an essentially conservative interpretation of the relationship between schools and society.

Historically, schools have been called on to mitigate the impact of political and economic events on society so that stability in the social order can be maintained. Urbanization, industrialization, and immigration caused schools to perform a number of functions: promote the American dream, facilitate social integration and cohesion, and advance homogeneity and uniformity in an increasingly diverse nation. Education's role typically has been the socialization of students into existing social, economic, and political ideologies.

This is not the only view of the role of schools in a democratic society, simply the dominant view. At the other end of the spectrum, critical theorists see schools as agents of change for society, as vehicles for social justice and public responsibility. In this view, the schools are active participants in the reconstruction and reinvention of a more effective social order.

As the "great cities" of our society deteriorate, the level of social integration and cohesion that fits a "melting pot" view of urban life is open to challenge. The gap between the rich and the poor in terms of disposable family income and the overall level of poverty in the United States exceeds that of all 10 countries included in the Luxembourg Income Study of six Western European countries, Canada, Australia, and Israel (Coder, Rainwater, and Smeeding 1989, pp. 322-23). Any contemporary school reform movement must examine alternative views of the social context of schooling in relation to: 1) the purposes of schooling, 2) the outcomes of schooling, and 3) the relation of schooling to other social service agencies.

Purposes of Schooling

Central to a discussion of school reform and the social contexts of schooling is the image that the reformer has of the role schools play in creating a better society.

Stability and Transformation

One contrasting set of beliefs is as follows:

Society uses education to contribute to the maintenance and stability of the social, economic, and political order.

OR

Society uses education to contribute to the improvement, growth, and transformation of the social order.

There is little doubt that during the past 20 years major national policy makers have seen education as a force to stabilize society. This traditional view of the relationship between education and the social order corresponds to a theoretical position described as the sociology of regulation (Burrell and Morgan 1979). The appeal of this position lies in the incremental posture it assumes toward change. Continual progress in the development of the social order is presumed to occur in an evolutionary and non-disruptive fashion. However, this traditional view of change, which focuses on maintaining the status quo, also functions to the disadvantage of significant segments of society, because it preserves and extends inequitable relationships. Convincing evidence exists that the gap between the poor and the rich in the United States has been widening for two decades.

24

The cogency of this issue for education in the 1990s is particularly acute, given the ever-increasing proportion of youngsters who are living in poverty and who thereby are separated from the mainstream of society. Clark and Astuto (1989*b*) warned of the establishment of a permanent underclass, citing the concentration of urban children who live in poverty, drop out of school, become functionally illiterate or marginal readers, and end up unemployed, on welfare, or in the criminal justice system. To avoid such outcomes requires abandoning inadequate educational programs that not only have failed to provide upward mobility, but also have fostered underachievement for the underclass.

Critical theorists argue that a sociology of radical change is necessary for redefining relationships so that all persons can participate fully in society. The sociology of radical change is discontinuous, because it involves not only the reallocation and redistribution of power but also the renegotiation and reformation of values and norms. The growing awareness that education reform has not been able to foster such social justice increases the press for radical change as a means of creating an equitable and just society.

The question of whether schools play a transformational or preservational role in society has been answered in the United States today; it is preservational. The question of whether the schools should serve a transformational or preservational role needs to be re-examined as an issue of ethics and morality. What is the responsibility of educational institutions, on the one hand, to protect society from the chaos of revolution while, on the other, to support the extension of the benefits of society to all children and youth? The means to resolve this dilemma are never self-evident. Human rights unfold from periods of darkness to light. Schools as agents of society are sometimes used to foster reform in the context of the sociology of regulation as, for example, in racial desegregation. In other cases, they become the instigator of reform, as they were in the expansion of educational opportunities for children with disabilities.

Today, many citizens and educators argue reasonably that the only hope of breaking the cycle of poverty, to which increasing millions seem doomed, lies in the transformation of the schools and society and in a transformational role for education in the process.

Commonality and Diversity

A related issue that is central to the purpose of schooling in society is whether schools are transmitters of a common heritage or active constructors of an ever-changing and diverse culture. These positions can be posed as:

> Schooling supports and promotes a common cultural heritage.

OR

> Schooling supports and promotes an understanding and appreciation of the diverse cultural traditions in American society.

The contention that schooling should support and promote a common cultural heritage grows out of the belief that the stability of society depends on a consensus of values and norms, the existence of shared language, and a common basis of experience. In its ordinary usage, the definition of the common school reflects this melting-pot concept of American culture. Because of an ethnocentric climate that has prevailed in American schools (and society), diverse cultural traditions have been sloughed off or devalued. This is illustrated by the silence in textbooks on the contributions of non-Western cultures and native or derivative American cultures, such as American Indian, Mexican-American, and African-American. Reagan asserted that Americanization often has involved more than just the acquisition of a common language and values; it has entailed the "absolute forgetfulness of all obligations or connections with other countries because of descent or birth" (1989, pp. 105-106). Giroux (1992) argued that the continued advocacy of an assimilationist approach by conservative reformers reflects a failure to rework dominant traditions in a changing context.

Even with the acknowledgment of cultural contributions and the incorporation of cultural traditions, such diversity usually is manifested in the form of add-ons to school curricula. At the most, diverse cultural traditions are acknowledged but relegated to a peripheral role in society. The voices and experiences of many children are silenced in the classroom when the tacit knowledge derived from the cultural resources that these students possess is not accessed (Willensky 1992). Although schooling provides requisite information and affirmation for members of the dominant culture, members of minority cultures "may find schooling irrelevant or even hostile to the development of cultural identities" (Cohen 1993, p. 293). When cultural frames of reference are in opposition to those of the mainstream, the minority student may experience either greater difficulty crossing the cultural boundaries at school or bicultural ambivalence toward home and school (Ogbu 1992).

The utility of a multicultural approach to schooling has benefits that extend far beyond minority students. As voice is given to cultures that have been marginalized, all students are empowered to invent contemporary cultural traditions that celebrate the diversity of our society. They begin to sense the strength of plural cultural traditions in the formation of knowledge, understanding, and possibilities for a new and richer cooperative society and common culture. The process of sharing novel cultural frames of reference becomes more important than reifying a narrow, dominant culture.

Outcomes of Schooling

The integral relationship of society to schools is never more clear than when the outcomes of schooling are discussed.

Determinism and Interruptability

Central to the discussion about this relationship is the extent to which the outcomes are determined by the socioeconomic status of students.

> Schools can effect only marginal, value-added gain in the education of students from differing economic and cultural backgrounds.

> **OR**

> Schools can interrupt the deterministic relationship of educational performance and socioeconomic status through in-school interventions.

Natriello, McDill, and Pallas (1990) traced the roots of this debate in their definition of the "educationally disadvantaged." They noted that over the past 35 years the scholarly community has moved from the concept of "cultural disadvantage," through a period that they describe as "educationally deprived," to the disadvantaged as "at-risk," to their working definition of the educationally disadvantaged:

> We view educational experiences as coming not only from formal schooling, but also from the family and community. Students who are educationally disadvantaged have been exposed to insufficient educational experiences in at least one of the three domains. (p. 13)

This strikes us as a useful definition, one consistent with the counter-assumption. However, Natriello and his colleagues presented evidence that the policy community at the national and state levels may be closer to the starting point than to the contemporary working definition. They described the two political and programmatic responses to the original concept of the culturally disadvantaged as 1) "educational policies emphasized the preschool years as a critical time, especially ages 3 and 4, when programs of 'planned enrichment' would serve to counteract the experiential inadequacies of the child's environment" and 2) "the growth of federally supported programs designed to make this population more like middle-class Americans" (p. 6). As far as we can see, the only change that has occurred in the past three decades is the locus of responsibility. Instead of the sole focus for Head Start being placed at the federal level, it is now the most popular state intervention. Instead of the growth of federally supported programs to remake the disadvantaged into middle-class Americans, this is now the emphasis of state and local practices and policies.

The most widespread, current, local, school reform movements are outdated. They are aimed at enhancing the value-added effect of schooling, but the result has produced a bifurcation in the purposes of education, differentiating students and allocating different kinds of education (Shea 1989). Students are placed in tracks that are designed to ameliorate the effects of their socioeconomic background. Although these differential educational experiences are determined by past achievement and are meant to anticipate future potential, they correlate with socioeconomic status. Therefore, because the track to which a student is assigned reflects the socioeconomic background of the student, the educational experiences to which he or she is exposed and the opportunities that become available as a result form a negative cycle from which few students escape.

Minority and low-socioeconomic students tend to be disadvantaged as a result of this cycle. Assessment plays a legitimizing role in disabling minority students by locating the problem with the child. Assessment insulates from scrutiny the schools, their programs, and the exclusionary attitudes of teachers toward the minority community (Cummins 1993).

The research that concluded that schooling does not make a substantial difference needs to be more vigorously debated at the levels of policy and practice. Such debate would foster an examination of how the structure and organization of schooling and the expectations of society contribute to this cycle and would lead to the consideration of alternative modes of organizing schools in order to contravene this self-fulfilling process. Acknowledging that effective schooling can successfully challenge the inevitability of low performance or failure in school by youth regardless of social, economic, and political conditions is a necessary first step toward successful schools for poor children and youth.

Family Deficit and Family Support

Beyond the issue of the deterministic effect of socioeconomic status on educational achievement is a more specific controversy about the family and alleged cultural deficits arising from the family. These lead to the following propositions:

> Factors such as poverty, minority status, and coming from atypical families place students at risk of failure in school.

> **OR**

> Regardless of socioeconomic status, ethnicity, or family background, most families value and support the education of their children.

There is no way to discuss the role of the family in supporting the education of children without discussing racism, gender bias, language dominance, and history. Neither policy makers nor school personnel are representative of the atypical families who are sending their children to school in ever-increasing numbers. Most minority parents have had unfortunate experiences in school and in their contact with governmental agencies and thus are reluctant to use the services of those agencies in their adult lives. School personnel must assume the initiative to revitalize the relationship between schools and communities and must open up the schools as safe places for parents. In some instances, this means rediscovering the sense of community that at one time centered on the local school.

Educators and policy makers cannot assume that the school failure of students from atypical families is attributable to family environments and lack of support systems. Such a belief, however erroneous, idealizes and romanticizes notions of mothering and parenting.

Alienation of school and community may occur as a result of a mismatch between a school culture that rewards competition and individual achievement and a community culture that values cooperation and group advancement (Cohen 1993). There are good reasons to adjust the competitiveness of the school culture for all children and, coincidentally, to respond to a least-served population. Ogbu (1992) described how involuntary minorities, those brought to the United States as slaves or indentured servants, have developed cultural differences to cope with their subordinate status. These differences are usually boundary-maintaining and in opposition to the dominant culture. The differences almost never are taken into account in adjusting school relationships with these parents.

A more obvious source of alienation is the high percentage of minority parents and grandparents who experienced failure in schools during their own youth, who do not know how to provide academic assistance or how to access the school, and who often are systematically excluded by school personnel from participation in schools.

None of these circumstances leads inevitably to ineffective relationships between the school and its clients. The choice is up to the schools, but many schools have chosen poorly. Cummins (1993) concluded that "dramatic changes in children's academic progress can be realized when educators take the initiative to change" (p. 109) exclusionary patterns into collaborative ones. Most minority parents have high aspirations for their children and want to ensure that the school provides the cultural capital necessary for success in the larger society (Delpit 1993).

Although it seems sensible to assume that familiarity with education systems has a great deal to do with a family's ability to shepherd their children through the system, a more accurate assertion is that the school's familiarity with and linkage to the community is more critical. One of the errors of relying on an overly simplistic explanation, such as the cultural deficit model, is that it leads educators to accept the inevitability of a poor match between family variables and schooling. This view deflects attention away from the responsibility of the school, social agencies, and private enterprise to provide effective programs to ameliorate the expected poor relationship. If, instead, educators operate on the assumption that, regardless of poverty, ethnicity, or family structure, there is natural variation in the ability of families to support the educational achievement of their children, then schools will be less constrained in the options they might consider for facilitating the achievement of all students.

Abandonment of the deficit model and acceptance of the proposition that minority parents value education as a means of economic viability and success in life for their children does not specify what parent

30

involvement means. Typically, for enlightened schools it has meant programs to orient parents to the schools — as the schools currently exist. Beyond that level, Epstein (1993) asserted that what is needed are "school and family partnerships" that emphasize information, communication, and participation (p. 715). She described "power-full partnerships" that stress equity and caring.

Fine (1993a) contended that the issue lies in modifying power relationships among educators, politicians, parents, and the public. She argued:

> Unless the dynamics of power are addressed, unless the range of and consequences of cultural capital are supported, and unless a deep vision of schools as community-based democracies of difference is engaged, parental involvement "projects" will be transformed into crisis intervention projects, into moments of having a voice but not getting a hearing, or into public contexts that slip into bankruptcy. (p. 707)

In Fine's view, "rich and real parental involvement requires a three-way commitment — to organizing parents, to restructuring schools and communities toward enriched educational and economic outcomes, and to inventing rich visions of educational democracies of difference" (p. 707). This conception does not rely on equity and caring relationships but on an actual transfer of power to parents in school communities and away from the school district bureaucracy. Aronowitz and Giroux (1994) concur with Fine's emphasis on power relationships:

> Returning schools to their public function means making families and communities co-owners in the schools. It means making democracy work through the process of sharing power, providing a democratic vision, and working collectively to create a multicultural and multiracial democracy. Schools abstracted from their communities diminish rather than enhance the public and civic functions of schooling. (p. 10)

Relation of Schooling to Social Service Agencies

The most conservative assumption about the school's role in relation to providing support services for children is that schools should concentrate only on the primary mission of educating students. However, this is an extremely limiting assumption and seems out of step with the impediments to children's learning created by social and economic conditions.

Segmented and Comprehensive Child and Family Support

Contemporary, conflicting assumptions are better represented as follows:

> To fulfill their educational mission, schools must cooperate with social and welfare agencies or form intersector organizational arrangements to provide child and youth services.

OR

> A unisector approach is required to provide a successful, comprehensive program for the education, nurturance, protection, growth, and development of children and youth.

Interorganizational arrangements (IOAs) have produced problems in both the private and public sectors. They are especially troublesome in the public arena, where the measure of leadership effectiveness is tied directly to the successful acquisition of budget, staff, and responsibility against competitor agencies. Each of the bureaucratic agencies asked to join an IOA seems immediately to be confronted with obstacles that will be perceived as reducing rather than enhancing its effectiveness.

Initially, the move to an IOA suggests past failure or inadequacy on the part of the participating agencies. IOAs are less stable environments within which each agency must function. Power is to be shared. Some agencies will be winners and others losers. Most will feel as if they have been losers. If the agency has been funded inadequately on its own, it will be likely to have more responsibility but no more funds in the IOA. The procedures of operation of each bureaucratic agency are now open to question. Issues of credit and blame will be reassessed. The percentage of an agency's scarce resources to be reallocated to IOA activity must be established. The level of coordination required, the amount of autonomy, and the resulting level of adaptability available to each agency are uncertain prior to the establishment of the joint venture (Gillespie and Mileti 1979).

Hodgkinson's (1989) accurate description of the steps that are required to establish a governmental joint venture are enough to reduce the enthusiasm of the participating agencies. Among other activities, the agencies must hold joint committee hearings in areas of interagency collaboration, fund projects across agencies and assign oversight accountability to joint committees, require joint budget presentations of agency leaders in interagency projects, and establish a common set of legislative-executive goals to be implemented across agencies, with accountability and timelines spelled out.

The viability of an alternative solution to social service delivery to children requires that it be as comprehensive as the social problems confronting the schools and sufficient to address children's multidimensional needs across social service areas. The invention of a unisector approach that focuses on providing a successfully integrated program to nurture, protect, and educate children, youth, and families would eliminate many of the problems that confound the interagency approach. However, as Fine cautioned, "supply-side interventions — changing people but not structures or opportunities — which leave unchallenged an inhospitable and discriminating economy and a thoroughly impoverished child care/social welfare system are inherently doomed to long-term failure" (1993*b*, p. 96). Polakow suggested engaging in a "politics of redistribution through a 'Children's Fund' that would be analogous to the social security system" (1992, p. 302).

A way of pursuing a unisector approach would be to create a single agency in which the sole focus would be the provision of all support services to children. The transfer of resources from existing agencies to a "new" agency, such as a Department of Children and Youth, would lessen the need for the unwieldy structures required by IOAs. However, even in this case Fine's warning is appropriate. An inadequately supported and funded Department of Children and Youth will fail, as the constituent agencies have failed, to provide a coordinated program of services required to support the country's children and youth.

Conclusion

The insidious effect of assumptions is the way they interconnect with and reify one another in a seemingly logical set of relationships. If one assumes that the maintenance of the social, economic, and political order should be a priority for education, then attempts by schools to counteract the fragmenting effects of diversity through the support and promotion of a common cultural tradition are appropriate. Similarly, the coupling of beliefs about social regulation and cultural uniformity sets in motion a self-fulfilling cycle of student failure, aided and abetted by limited expectations for the outcomes of educational interventions. Subscribing to a deficit model of cultural, parental, and community resources and values further restricts the number of allies that educators can call on for support. Overwhelmed by the scope of the school's responsibilities in today's society and by the severely limited resources devoted to education, educators further dilute their energies and resources in interagency collaboration.

On the other hand, if educators begin with a belief in the transformative role of education, the value of accessing diversity, a faith in the potential success of every student, and a commitment to collaborative and political linkages with parents and communities, then mustering the inventiveness to create new ways of organizing on behalf of children will be the logical, moral, and just thing to do.

CHAPTER THREE

ASSUMPTIONS ABOUT THE STRUCTURAL CONTEXT OF SCHOOLING

Pragmatic attempts to design school organizational structures that are responsive to the developmental needs of children and youth and sensitive to the demands of adults for freedom and support are constrained by the assumptions and beliefs that ground the redesign process. These assumptions and beliefs become "givens" that direct new designs, narrow the range of options considered to be feasible, and dull the imagination. Some of these assumptions are rooted in dominant perspectives about the necessary features of organizations.

Bringing groups of people together in a common setting with common purposes produces dilemmas that are inherent in collective work. Organizations are collectivities with a wide range of individual, common, and external purposes. How do we structure workplaces in ways that are responsive to professional demands, local contingencies, the needs of production, and the competing choices that swirl around us? How do we think about the structures that will help us do our work in environments that respect the individual and that support growth and development? What structures do we build to contend with the persistent and natural conditions of conflict, ambiguity, and dissonance that accompany collective efforts? How do we think about the outcomes or products of our individual and collective work?

Bureaucracy has become the universally accepted pattern for structuring workplaces. The principles and elements of bureaucracy represent administrative choices designed to increase organizational efficiency. The values, beliefs, and assumptions supportive of bureaucracy are disputable, but rarely disputed. Identifying these assumptions, assessing their fit with the purposes of schools and districts, and recognizing the trade-offs that have been hidden by their acceptance are prerequisites to creating new organizational designs.

Organizational analysis ordinarily is conducted according to the basic elements of bureaucracy, including hierarchy of office, rules regulating the conduct of offices, division of labor among organizational positions, and an impersonal orientation based on rational decisions grounded in facts, not feelings. Using this framework as an analytic tool reifies the elements of bureaucracy and blurs the larger critical issues that bureaucracy is argued to address: 1) coordination of work, 2) relationships among workers, and 3) individual and organizational productivity.

Coordination of Work

One of the first concerns confronted in the design of organizational structures is the identification of mechanisms to ensure coordinated work. At an intuitive level, the possibility of people falling all over each other, stepping on each other's toes, overlooking some important aspect of work, or duplicating efforts raises an image of chaos. Bureaucratic structure provides one set of choices to counter these problems:

- Establish a point of authority and responsibility within the organization (the hierarchy of authority).
- Specify the work roles of individuals (division of labor and task specification).
- Routinize decision making (rules and regulations).
- Ground organizational action in rationality (impersonal orientation).
- Implement processes that routinize planning, organization, staffing, decision making, reporting, and budgeting according to the principles of bureaucracy.

Bureaucracy and Democracy

The assumptions underlying bureaucracy represent one way to coordinate collective work. Alternative assumptions reveal other possibilities:

Formalization of power relationships, specification of work responsibilities, and implementation of organizing processes consistent with these principles establish the conditions for coordinated work.

OR

Democratic structures that promote individual responsibility, shared activities, and implementation of processes consistent with principles of social justice and individual growth and development establish the conditions for coordinated work.

Bureaucracy as an organizational form has few proponents. The "red tape" is aggravating. The unresponsiveness to internal preferences and external demands is troubling. The routinization of work is stultifying. However, bureaucracy persists in schools, districts, unions, government, public agencies, and private corporations. Why? One answer is acceptance of the assumptions on which bureaucratic structures are built. The buck should stop somewhere, and so formal organizational roles are important. Someone has to be in charge, thus power relationships are necessary. Stability has to be maintained, thus the processes of organization need to be institutionalized. While bureaucracy may be seen as an annoyance, at best, and destructive of human talent, at worst, its coordinative elements and mechanisms are viewed as necessary. But are they necessary? Do bureaucratic coordinative mechanisms stimulate attention to the work and common purposes of the organization?

The formalization of power relationships distracts attention from the technical core of the organization's work and focuses attention on management forms. Written communication of policies and procedures constrains the discretionary authority of individual decision makers to respond to daily events. Power relationships are played out in disciplinary procedures, incentive programs, and evaluation systems that clarify the range of behaviors expected from workers. Structures and layers are added in an effort to be ever more clear and precise about power, authority, and responsibility.

In schools, for example, the professional discretion of teachers to make decisions about individual students or about the values on which a learning community might be built is severely curtailed. Teacher work is specified in terms of role and task responsibilities, rather than principles of teaching and learning. The layering of authority relationships reinforces the isolation of teachers in their classrooms because it attends to the individual's place in the hierarchy and not to the professional linkages that support collaboration and shared responsibility. Some observers assert that teachers do not want broad responsibility outside the classroom. That observation misses a critical point: In an environment of power relationships and job specificity, individualism is the only reasonable response.

The structures imposed by a bureaucratic framework assume an external locus of control. This attention to the control of workers and work by management diminishes recognition of individual creativity and efficacy. Management control ignores the fact that organizations are social contexts. Meaning is arrived at by the participants in interaction with each other and with other stakeholders. Bureaucratic theory consigns this basic feature of organizational life to the "informal organization." The resulting opposition of the formal and informal not only fragments the collectivity but, more importantly, it treats the social interaction and, consequently, the social construction of organizational reality as "noise" in the system. Formalization of power relationships is needed to bring the purposes and aspirations of workers into line with management. Instead of coordinating talent, formalizing power relationships blocks creative responses and adaptation to changing circumstances.

Organizational processes maintain the stability of the bureaucratic form. Planning, organizing, staffing, decision making, reporting, and budgeting are bound by bureaucratic principles and, simultaneously, reinforce and implement them. The key players hold hierarchic positions of authority. In almost all instances, the reactions and ideas of others are sought. Teachers, students, and parents — or their representatives — are given opportunities for input. "Input" means information or preferences in the form of advice to the decision maker. Teachers and parents have little real decision-making authority; students have almost none. Consequently, formal decision making occurs far from the action in schools. And informal decision making is private, isolated, and idiosyncratic.

This is not to say that the bureaucratic framework does not serve as a powerful force to coordinate organizational work; merely that it is inherently imperfect. The bureaucratic framework trades off individual talent and responsibility for routinization in the name of coordination. First, the combination of hierarchic positions of authority and division of labor intentionally fragment the organization. Consequently, workers who make numerous decisions around the technical core are unable to communicate those decisions widely and are unable to routinely and easily influence broader work decisions. At the same time, managers become more removed from the technical core and begin to see the primary work of the organization as if they were outsiders.

Second, the hierarchy establishes classes of individuals with more or less official capacity to influence their own work and the work of the collective. Obviously, a small "ruling class" has more influence; a worker class has less. The hierarchy of authority is a mechanism of subordination. Subordination is intended to reduce individual freedom — and it does.

Third, as a result of this "class system" within organizations, managers and administrators (and people engaged in research about them) become caught up in defining and redefining the meaning of leadership. This attention to meaning is important in a system of subordination. Images of leadership are caught up in the role of designated leaders over people.

Abandoning a bureaucratic form does not mean abandoning coordination. Schools, as well as other types of organizations, are powerful behavior settings. Norms of human interaction and the nature of work foster continuity and a sense of stability. The routine of polity (the natural condition of organized activity) establishes standards for individual and collective action. The wisdom of people safeguards the individual and the group from acting against their own best interests. The natural inclination of people to bracket organizational events in simple (sometimes simplistic) ways as they make sense of the organization suggests orderliness, not chaos (Weick 1979). Organizations would not run wild if bureaucracy were abandoned. The strength of the behavior setting, the routine of polity, the wisdom of people, and the natural search for order are strong forces for continuity (Clark and Astuto 1988, pp. 126-28). Consequently, the coordination of collective work can flow easily from alternative assumptions and value premises that hold more promise.

Democratic structures open possibilities for coordinative strategies that are more attentive to the technical core of the organization's work and more appreciative of the talents of all participants. Instead of assuming that a system of control and subordination is a necessary coordinative mechanism, democracy recognizes that the individual is the critical building block of collective life.

Individuals with equal formal power are as concerned about ways of ensuring smooth operations as are superordinates in hierarchical structures. The strategic difference is a shift in the principles, beliefs, and values that drive coordination. Cooperative and collaborative structures characterize self-governing work groups. The basis for collaboration is found in the work of the organization — teaching and learning, in the case of schools.

Broad distribution of power and authority unlocks organizational adaptation and responsiveness. The conventional wisdom that the buck has to stop somewhere reflects the reality that most organizational participants do not have the power or authority to exercise discretion when confronted with a problem or dilemma. For example, disgruntled patrons want to talk to a manager (or a principal) because they believe that the manager has the authority to do something. Often the complainant arrives at the manager's desk because other individuals in the organization have been constrained by the hierarchy from making decisions on their own.

Democratic mechanisms that provide for collective decisions about the limits of individual discretion promote individual responsibility for and connectedness to organization-wide problems and demands. Diffusion of responsibility increases acceptance of accountability among organizational participants. The formulaic authority-task structure, which is a necessary feature of the bureaucratic framework, gives way to a social-professional environment focused on the organization's work rather than on control of the organization's workers.

Relationships Among Workers

Just as the concern of neophyte teachers is classroom order and discipline, the concern of beginning principals is organizational order and discipline.

Control and Empowerment

Organizational structure is a critical force that shapes relationships among workers. Patterns of interaction among teachers, administrators, students, parents, and community members are facilitated or constrained by choices about the structural design of schools. Assumptions about collective work drive choices about the structure. For example:

> Goals, specification of task assignments, and decision making grounded in impersonality promote fairness, reduce interpersonal conflict, and optimize organizational control.

> **OR**

> Norms and ethics of professional practice and decision making grounded in values of social justice and responsibility promote equity, tolerate conflict, and optimize individual control.

Traditional assumptions about relationships among people in work environments reflect a belief that conflict is an organizational pathology that can be reduced if the sources of conflict are eliminated. When people come together to accomplish common purposes, disagreements inevitably arise about: 1) what work or outcomes should be the focus of attention, 2) who is responsible for which aspects of the organiza-

40

tion's work, and 3) whether decisions about individuals and their work are characterized by favoritism or fairness. Organizational goals, job specifications, and rational, impersonal decision making reduce the ambiguity and uncertainty likely to generate conflicts. But do they promote fairness?

Organizational goals are not sensitive to individual goals and so mute interesting and provocative differences. The point of goals is to cohere the intention of all participants, leaders and followers. The leadership role of the administrator includes identifying the organization's vision, mission, and goals, and working with others to achieve consensus about them. However, organizational purposes are numerous, complex, and often conflicting. In order to achieve consensus in a traditional organization, goals are developed at an abstract level at or near the apex of the organization's hierarchy. The conflict and debate that would flow from the trade-offs that occur in prioritizing some purposes and de-emphasizing others are ignored. Consequently, such goals are weak indicators of the beliefs of some participants, some of the time, about some aspects of the organization's work.

Work is shaped by a wide range of personal, professional, and organizational demands and constraints that have much more meaning for the individual than a set of relatively abstract statements agreed on at some distance from the site of action. Consequently, organizational goals do little to capture the imagination or interest of most people. They are more likely to provoke disdain and disengagement, rather than respect and commitment.

Clear, precise work roles interfere with the development of classroom practice based on professional expertise and collaborative action. Numerous factors affect how individuals think about their work. Undoubtedly, one is the organization's description of work responsibilities. More important, teachers also make sense of their work based on professional norms and experiences. In schools, confusion and dissatisfaction increase when the teacher's work and working conditions do not reflect beliefs and expectations about teaching that have been acquired through experience, study, and inquiry. Additionally, the more powerful meaning of work is constructed in interaction with others, such as co-workers, students, and other stakeholders in the organization's work. Clear, precise work roles are much less important on a day-to-day basis than the norms and expectations that emerge in actual work. The trade-off between specification and individual initiative has a negative effect on professional performance.

Impersonal systems of rules, regulations, and standard operating procedures distract attention from the unique contributions of individuals and ignore organizational responsibility for the well-being of all workers. The importance of impersonality in the workplace is argued on the grounds that it is a sensible alternative to favoritism. If everyone in the workplace is subject to the same rules, regulations, and standard operating procedures, then no one can assert advantage within the system. Accepting for the moment that these impersonal systems actually are implemented, they miss the point that workers are not all the same and that the conditions in which they work are often ambiguous. Impersonality takes the administrator "off the hook." The difficult decisions are those that require differential responses that support growth, development, and a sense of the creativity and efficacy of individuals. Treating everyone the same does not ensure fairness. However, treating everyone the same does reduce the ability of the administrator to support individual initiative.

Bureaucratic principles offer inherently imperfect options for promoting positive relationships among workers. First, the primacy of organizational goals and carefully specified position descriptions routinize the work of individuals in organizations. This routinization negatively affects both the workers and the organization. For workers, daily responsibilities can become dull and uninteresting. For the organization, current work forms become institutionalized at the expense of innovative new practices.

Second, goals simultaneously direct attention to some purposes and away from others. The nature of consensus and the history of organizations lead to the prediction that goals are more likely to advantage the powerful and disadvantage those already poorly served. Consequently, an over-reliance on building consensus around goals perpetuates inequities.

Third, bureaucratic impersonality impedes the development of community. People experience the organization differently. Women and men, children and adults, insiders and outsiders see and feel organizational life from quite different perspectives. An impersonal orientation ignores differences. Abandoning the bureaucracy is necessary to recognize alternative assumptions about the relationships among people in organizations.

Conflict is a natural condition in organizations. Schools experience relatively high levels of ambiguity that flow from competing preferences, conflicting work demands, and unclear technologies surrounding the technical core — teaching and learning. In a structural context that views conflict as a pathology, debates surrounding the technical core never become joined. Professional staff resolve dilemmas privately, isolated from their colleagues. Norms of nonintrusiveness emerge that relieve professional staff of the responsibility of confronting ineffective or inappropriate practices. Responsibility is centralized with administrators, who intervene more or less regularly in the professional practice of teachers.

While bureaucratic structures intimidate and isolate teachers and reduce their freedom to respond creatively to the challenges of their work, alternative structures that view conflict and debate as natural conditions encourage competing perspectives and individual responsibility for group action. Opportunities for teachers and support staff to discuss individual students and alternative possibilities for curriculum and instruction are a regular part of the work day. Decision-making mechanisms revolve more intensely around teaching, learning, and the growth and developmental needs of students. In short, more "space" is provided for meaningful professional debate, which is centered on teaching and learning.

More likely than not, when flexible structures that promote professional debate and decision making are implemented, school climate will decline temporarily. One reason for this decline is that definition and assessment of climate reflect the dominant assumptions. Another reason is that higher levels of professional interaction and more public professional practice are personally challenging. The challenge and effort pay off, however, in the creation of vibrant workplaces, in more thoughtful professional practice, and in school contexts that are more responsive to students.

A community of workers replaces goals, job specifications, and impersonality in the workplace with respect and support for individuals that are based on the norms and ethics of professional practice. *Community* is defined as a unified body, individuals with a common interest. The particular focus of schools is the development of learning communities. The links among individuals — students, teachers, administrators, parents, community members — are teaching and learning, growth and development. Teaching and learning are responsive to individual strengths and needs. Learning communities develop norms, beliefs, and practices that foster growth and understanding. Equity is promoted because everyone is recognized for his or her individuality and unique contribution to the community.

The idea of community requires development; otherwise, it becomes merely a romanticized vision of shared values. Schools responsive to diverse populations and accepting of competing perspectives are communities of difference that foster a sense of individual agency, that is, the ability to make a difference. Learning communities of difference support individual action and growth by providing a safe space to voice ideas and opinions, coupled with accountability for that expression. The unity of community arises from an ethical referent, for example, social justice. Consequently, learning communities of difference are not built on sameness or agreement. What binds the community together is the value premise that guides action and debate.

Individual and Collective Productivity

People join organizations for many reasons — to be of service to others, to contribute to the well-being of society, to have something interesting to do, and to support themselves. Organizations also have multiple reasons for existing; and, when pressed, organization stakeholders can develop long lists of hoped-for outcomes.

High Standards and Improved Processes

Traditional assumptions narrow consideration of organizational effectiveness by specifying outcomes that can be monitored and assessed; alternative assumptions focus on organizational processes.

> Performance standards and assessment strategies ensure high-quality organizational outcomes.

> **OR**

> Improved organizational processes ensure high-quality organizational outcomes.

When concerns are raised about organizational productivity, traditional assumptions result in efforts to standardize and monitor performance. System-level performance standards are centralized and dominated by administrators. Consequently, these standards represent narrow organizational concerns, tend to be linear and unidimensional, and create winners and losers.

Performance standards assume that lack of productivity is explained by the unwillingness of individuals to achieve high levels of performance. Overemphasizing standards and assessment turns organizational resources and energies toward documenting failure. The strategy for improvement is to pinpoint those areas in which individuals are not performing. The next step is remedial. Two problems with this kind of thinking are obvious. First, the result is a form of "blaming the victim." Children and youth most at risk of school failure are the explanation for the failure of schools. Second, blaming individuals distracts attention from the organizational processes that reinforce failure. Scarce resources — time, money, and energy — are used in ways least likely to generate improvement, for example, complicated and burdensome personnel evaluation systems.

Organizational participants believe that assessment strategies lack validity, reliability, and credibility. This includes both professional evaluation and student assessment. Personnel evaluation systems are typically viewed by participants as inaccurate representations of individual work and accomplishments. Individuals with a sense of self-efficacy rate themselves quite high on performance in relation to their colleagues. Simultaneously, evaluation by a supervisor is believed only if it matches the subordinate's own evaluation. Disparities between the two evaluations result in job dissatisfaction. Consequently, evaluation systems do little to spur improvement unless everyone is in agreement about the quality of an individual's work. However, they do much to reduce norms of sharing and collaboration.

Similarly, assessment of students through standardized performance testing generates more problems than improvements. Test construction drives curriculum and instruction. Despite evidence of technical reliability and validity, teachers complain that tests do not measure what they teach. The dominant assumption about the merits of performance standards and assessment is so strong that the focus of reform is to design better assessments. Alternative strategies for organizational improvement that build on the experiences of practitioners and focus on improved processes, rather than better product measurement, are ignored.

Organizational accomplishment means increasing the number of winners, while performance standards and assessment strategies focus on identifying the losers. Achievers build on strengths. Successful individuals develop a sense of their own capabilities through successful experiences. Systems that identify losers, with clear evidence of the extent of their failure, violate principles of effective teaching and learning. Alternative perspectives focus on developing a learning community characterized by individual confidence and success.

Improvement processes that are likely to make a difference in the quality of work in the organization are responsive to emerging conditions. Formative and participatory evaluation of collective work recognizes spontaneous success and views uncertainty and ambiguity as natural phenomena. Innovation requires room for playfulness and individual creativity, which are suppressed by standardized practice and performance monitoring.

Improvement means getting better at what we do rather than getting better at measuring the quality of our products. The long and interesting tradition of research and experience with school improvement demonstrates that people are the key to organizational success. In schools, a change in practice requires a change in beliefs, curriculum, and pedagogy. Organizations that have the capacity to improve are supported by organizational structures and beliefs that focus attention on the organization's work and workers. Structural contexts characterized by freedom, responsiveness, and responsibility are necessary prerequisites to improved professional practice.

Individual improvement flows from success and increased personal capacity. The difference between building strength and identifying weakness is subtle. Physical fitness provides a useful analogy. When people work out, they improve their fitness, which in turn allows them to work harder and improve more. Success feeds success. Effective teachers do the same thing. Students who become convinced of their ability develop a sense of academic efficacy. They commit to learning in large part because they have experienced success in learning.

Professionals in responsible organizations are accountable to themselves, their clients, the organization's stakeholders, and the public. Decentralizing power and authority and eschewing externally imposed performance standards and monitoring systems do not mean ignoring individual and collective accountability. To the contrary, professional educators act in the public interest and with the public's trust. Responsible action requires them to ask introspective questions about their own practice and to assess the learning activities and options available to students. Teachers and administrators become responsible, under these conditions, for finding ways of communicating regularly with a wide range of interested stakeholders; and they design sensible, practical strategies for their stakeholders to obtain and contribute information. As a result, accountability becomes a component of the structural context of the school, not an externally driven, narrow, or primarily symbolic event.

Conclusion

The assumptions and beliefs supportive of a bureaucratic framework dominate thinking about the organizational context of schools. Yet a bureaucratic framework represents only one set of choices for dealing with the major concerns of coordinated work, relationships among people, and productivity. Frameworks for viewing organizational realities can serve as lenses or blinders. In the case of the bureaucratic framework, the underlying assumptions compete with basic principles about teaching and learning. The trade-offs are costly: freedom for control, educational processes for order and managerial simplicity, equity for procedural fairness, substantive accountability for performance standards.

Bureaucracy has proven to be a persistent and pervasive organizational form. Challenges to the underlying assumptions of bureaucracy yield provocative, promising alternatives. Those alternatives involve more than the elimination of the more-offensive bureaucratic elements. Inventing new structures requires ingenuity and experimentation.

CHAPTER FOUR

ASSUMPTIONS ABOUT THE INDIVIDUAL WITHIN THE SCHOOL CONTEXT

People are the reason for organizational failure, or people are the source of organizational success. These and other assumptions about people in the workplace are reflected in contemporary education reform strategies. For example, recent reforms in teacher education include increased requirements for initial certification, ongoing participation in professional development activities for recertification, extended field experiences, inservice support systems for new teachers, and the formation of the National Board for Professional Teaching Standards. These reforms reveal beliefs that teaching is a professional activity and that professionals responsible for the growth and development of children need advanced levels of expertise.

On the other hand, some states have reduced the requirements for initial certification of teachers, even including, at the extreme, alternative routes that reflect the belief that schools would be improved if talented people who have not chosen teaching as a career could be recruited into the teaching profession. These latter recruits are not required to commit themselves to advanced training nor to demonstrate the same level of professional expertise as those who have selected teaching as a career. Their preparation is "on-the job" with emphasis on mentorships and practice-oriented instruction, in the manner of an apprenticeship.

The public and policy makers (and perhaps education practitioners themselves) are puzzled about how to think about teachers and teaching. Are teachers experts or skilled technicians? Are they objects of public trust or targets for suspicion? Are they the reason for school failure or the hope for school improvement?

And what about students? What explains their varying levels of engagement in and curiosity about learning?

Assumptions about the people who populate schools — teachers, support staff, administrators, students — shape practice, sometimes subtly, sometimes obviously and intentionally. Understanding the conventional assumptions about individuals within the school context and exploring alternative assumptions are critical prerequisites to designing meaningful education reforms. These assumptions cluster around three major areas of concern and confusion: 1) motivation, 2) ability, and 3) level and type of contribution to organizational outcomes.

Motivation

People exert energy toward achieving individual and organizational purposes. Why? What explains variations in levels of engagement in work? Motivation is a complicated and multidimensional concept that is confusing when applied in the workplace.

External and Internal Motivation

Beliefs about motivation are learned through experience, through popular theoretical frameworks, and through research about organizations. And, of course, different perspectives yield different insights:

> Individuals are motivated to achieve institutional objectives by incentives.

> **OR**

> Individuals are self-motivated to achieve institutional objectives unless blocked by the organizational environment.

The assumption that people are externally motivated is rooted in traditional views about people in the workplace. Traditional perspectives recognize the existence of an informal organization comprised of the purposes, needs, and aspirations of workers. Yet management is urged to subordinate these purposes, needs, and aspirations whenever they conflict with predetermined organizational objectives. Thus from a bureaucratic standpoint, the formal organization matters; the informal organization is "noise in the system."

McGregor (1960) observed that much of managerial practice reflects a management belief that workers, left to their own initiative, are not interested in quality performance. Designated as Theory X, this managerial perspective posits:

1. People inherently dislike work and will avoid it whenever possible.
2. People must be directed and coerced to put forth adequate effort toward the achievement of organizational objectives.
3. People prefer to be directed and to avoid responsibility (McGregor 1960, pp. 33-34).

These bald assertions of Theory X might seem too extreme to have relevance to discussions of contemporary education reforms. Yet most recent efforts to restructure and reform schools are guided by these assumptions.

State monitoring and accountability systems reflect a concern that local educators will not work hard enough to support student learning unless coerced. Promotion of national achievement tests reflects a lack of trust that state and local educators will select the wisest instruction unless the preferred outcomes are specified. National statements of educational goals, state identification of a common core of knowledge, and local administrative efforts to articulate a clear vision of the purposes of the school all assume that teachers and principals prefer or need to have their professional lives externally controlled.

These reforms reflect similar beliefs about students: 1) testing will result in students working harder, 2) an agreed-on curricular core will attract the attention of students to important knowledge, and 3) students need to have their days structured by adults. Relationships between teachers and students, and principals and students, especially those interactions routinized by school rules, also reflect the belief that improved student performance requires the use of "carrots and sticks."

An assumption that motivation requires incentives and control mechanisms conflicts with motivation theory and principles of human growth and development. For example, Maslow's (1943/1987) theory of motivation contends that people progress through a hierarchy of human needs, from needs for basic physical requirements to safety to affiliation to esteem to self-actualization. The idea that human beings strive for personal fulfillment is quite different than the belief that human beings are lethargic, unmotivated, and uninterested in their own growth and achievement.

Even more to the point, Herzberg's (1976) theory and research on motivation argue that basic physical needs are not relevant as motivators in the workplace. External incentives such as salary, safety, and relationships with administrators are sources of dissatisfaction when they are inadequate; but they are not sources of motivation. Motivators are linked to personal growth and achievement, such as individual responsibility for work, recognition of individual contributions to the organization, and the challenges of the work itself. This is consistent with McGregor's Theory Y view of people:

1. Physical and mental effort in work is as natural as play or rest.

2. People will exercise self-direction and self-control in the service of objectives to which they are committed.

3. Commitment to objectives is a function of the rewards associated with their achievement and the most significant rewards (satisfaction of ego and self-actualization needs) can be products of efforts directed toward organizational objectives.

4. People not only accept but also seek responsibility.

5. Imagination, ingenuity, and creativity in solving organizational problems is widely, not narrowly, distributed in the population (McGregor 1960, pp. 47-48).

The assumption that people are self-motivated is supported by more than motivation theory and research. It is also consistent with the reports of teachers that the intrinsic rewards of teaching — reaching a child, seeing growth and development, fostering learning — are most relevant to them. Self-motivation also is characteristic of young people. Research about students' thought processes has focused on reinforcement, the need for achievement, locus of control, and students' understandings of themselves as learners (Wittrock 1986, pp. 304-306). This literature demonstrates the importance of the student's responsibility for learning and sense of efficacy as a learner. As children mature, their capacity for self-direction increases. Yet they often find themselves in even more-controlled learning environments that take away their expanding sense of initiative and curiosity.

Responsibility for motivating others mirrors the hierarchy of power and authority. Within the school context, teachers motivate students; principals motivate teachers. Apparently, the higher an individual is in the administrative hierarchy, the more credit he or she is given for being self-motivated and self-directed. This linkage between motivation, control, and power highlights another interesting observation made by McGregor. To the extent that it is true that individuals in subordinate roles avoid responsibility or lack ambition, such avoidance would appear to be a consequence of limited opportunity and experience, not an inherent human characteristic (McGregor 1960, p. 48).

Competition and Cooperation

What types of work environments sustain an individual's sense of motivation? Two assumptions help frame this discussion:

Competition stimulates individuals to higher levels of individual achievement.

OR

Cooperation provides the nurturance, support, and collegiality that stimulate individual achievement.

Competition is highly valued in American society. But does it sustain individual self-motivation in the workplace? The argument in support of competition is based on the assumption that one's personal best is achieved when the individual is pushed beyond current ability and skill levels by the heat of competition. As early as the pre-World War I era of scientific management, Taylor (1916/1987) argued that competitive work environments stimulate productivity. In factories, this notion was operationalized as piece-work; in professional work, it takes the form of comparative measures of individual performance in relation to organizational outcomes.

Establishing competitive environments in schools is at the heart of many personnel policies. Fascination with merit pay and recognition programs for teachers is based on a belief that directly connecting work and rewards will yield increased teacher effort to improve student achievement. Testing programs to monitor student achievement and compare classrooms, schools, or districts establish conditions for identifying winners and losers.

Despite popular beliefs, competition may not create the most productive conditions for individual achievement. A counter-argument is that self-motivation is sustained when individuals maintain a sense of self-efficacy and work in a context in which people (teachers, administrators, students, parents) help each other to develop skills, to take risks, and to challenge standard operating procedures. Competitive environments isolate people; cooperative environments bring people together and protect diversity of experience, preference, and interest.

School improvement, like individual learning, is an interactive, mutually reinforcing activity that requires the collaborative efforts of all participants. Cooperation is enhanced by personal actions and organizational support. Thus to build cooperative environments, individuals need to exhibit cooperation in both language and action. Simultaneously, organizational support needs to signal the benefits of cooperation for collective purposes.

Cooperative work environments characterize high-producing organizations because they:

- foster sharing of ideas,
- allow idiosyncrasy to be a strength rather than a weakness,
- support innovation and change, and
- extend the range of perspectives on work problems.

The question for restructuring and reforming schools is, What organizational form is compatible with the demands of cooperative work environments? Bureaucratic structures isolate individuals and organize work around principles of efficiency, authority, and procedural specificity; they both establish and support competition, for which they were originally designed. The concept of community, on the other hand, values shared efforts in an environment that is safe for individual difference and experimentation. Structures built on principles of community establish and support the condition of cooperation.

Organizational structures consistent with the principles of community are particularly relevant for schools. The work of schools involves three major dimensions: 1) the professional community, 2) learning communities, and 3) the stakeholder community. Structures supportive of the professional community provide time for dialogue and access to ideas, both within the narrower school community and throughout the broader professional arena of practitioners in other schools, colleagues in higher education, education researchers, and professional associations. Structures supportive of learning communities provide opportunities for interaction and caring between teachers and students and among students in collaborative learning activities. Structures supportive of the stakeholder community provide for collaboration and enhance communication among parents, area citizens, local businesses, and agencies that provide child and family support.

Motivation and personality theories and research demonstrate over and over again that people inherently are drawn to learning, work, and responsibility. Barnard (1938), Argyris (1957), and McGregor (1960) described with force and eloquence the wide range of talents and positive predilections that people bring to their work. Yet dominant beliefs about motivation continue to view people as organizational problems in the making and fail to recognize that the real source of organizational problems may be the bureaucratic form.

Ability

McGregor suggested that the talents and intellectual abilities of people are only partially used at work. Policy makers and reformers have introduced a number of initiatives to create conditions to increase the performance levels of teachers and students.

Technicians and Professionals

These reforms reflect different ways of thinking about individual ability:

> Outstanding educators demonstrate high levels of technical skill.

> **OR**

> Outstanding educators demonstrate high levels of professional expertise.

Everyone agrees that the work of teachers is the critical element of effective schooling. However, not everyone agrees on the nature of that work. Does it involve essentially the mastery of specific technical skills or the development of a professional repertoire of instructional options, in-depth understanding of the content of instruction, sensitivity to the wide range of student needs, and comprehensive understanding of the principles of child and adolescent growth and development?

These competing beliefs are played out in the choice of reforms in preservice teacher education, inservice programs for teacher development, and improvement of school and classroom practice. The reforms in teacher education mirror the limitations of vision and possibility found in school reform. Most preparation programs continue to be undergraduate degree programs with little intellectual, or temporal, space for intense professional preparation. And teacher preparation programs are spread among 1,300 colleges and universities, many of which commit few resources and low energy to these programs.

Continuing education is an essential characteristic for all professional fields. Yet some states have narrowed the range of growth possibilities by expanding coursework requirements in the basic disciplines for recertification and reducing or eliminating coursework in professional education, an arbitrary and unnecessary choice between bodies of necessary skills and knowledge. Many school districts rely on "inservice days" — often devoted merely to sharing information about district-directed initiatives — as their program for professional development.

While effective organizations in the private sector expand their investment in staff development, school districts have reduced staff-development expenditures at a time when the challenges of teaching have become more complex.

In the classroom, significant variation occurs: 1) in the amount of time teachers spend on different subjects, 2) in the instructional focus on basic skills or higher-order thinking skills, 3) in the amount of teacher direction, 4) in the quality of instructional materials, and 5) in the level of responsiveness to an individual student's needs. Evidence exists of wide variability in the quality of instruction for poor children, children of color, children with special needs, and girls, in contrast to the instruction of white males.

Most popular initiatives to improve teaching are based on a belief that teaching is a technical skill. The technical dimensions of teaching involve the delivery of curricular content, implementation of instructional methods, administration of assessment strategies to gauge student learning, and application of methods of classroom control. Reforms such as outcomes-based education reflect these dimensions and, consequently, teacher discretion is narrowed to ensure precise implementation of technical skills.

Rather than establish conditions that maximize the abilities of teachers, tightly linked instructional packages stunt performance, growth, imagination, and community. They are examples of McGregor's observation that, although people are naturally self-motivated, organizational factors often serve to depress individual ingenuity and achievement. This point was illustrated clearly by Argyris (1957). Based on a synthesis of the literature about human growth and development, Argyris concluded that organizational work environments demand less-mature behavior from adults. Controlling, hierarchical, bureaucratic environments are more congruent with less-mature behaviors, including passivity, dependence, few capabilities, shallow interests, short time perspective, subordinate position, and lack of self-control and awareness.

As enacted in schools, these structures also produce a debilitating effect on students. Not only do they socialize students to view work as dull and constraining, they also rein in the natural curiosity of children and youth. For too many students, schools are not exciting, lively places that engender enthusiasm for and engagement in learning and academic pursuits.

An alternative assumption about the work and abilities of educators is based on a belief that outstanding teaching requires professional expertise. Professionals draw from a broad range of relevant disciplines to make decisions about the conduct of professional practice. Teams of staff work together to determine the wisest course of instruction for students. Some efforts to restructure schools — those that provide teachers with opportunities to make professional decisions about their work and about activities to support student learning — require a definition of ability that incorporates professional expertise.

Viewing teachers as members of a professional community focuses attention on norms of collegiality (Little 1982) and the ethics of professional practice. This shift has implications for the work of principals. Sources of control are within the processes of professional work and collaboration, not in the hierarchy of authority. Administrative actions focused on stability, goal setting, regularity, accountability, intervention, control, and efficiency are either redundant or destructive, or both, of cooperation and community. Alternative actions that support the professional community, the learning community, and the stakeholder community require more complex, professional expertise on the part of the principal. Facilitating the working communities of the school requires practices that foster activity, the development of a professional community that incorporates diversity, variability in work processes and structures, individual efficacy, and empowerment of staff and students (Clark and Astuto 1988).

Under these conditions, principals provide support to the professional community by working collaboratively to design, critique, and improve structures and reinvigorate the norms of professional practice. They provide support for the learning community by working with staff and students to implement a wide range of learning activities. They support the stakeholder community by working outside the school, creating links with families, social agencies, and political structures. In short, they support the school's internal communities and serve as the school's representative to the larger communities and outside agencies.

Evaluation and Collaborative Learning

Different ways of thinking about the work of teachers and administrators are accompanied by different ways of establishing the conditions for improvement:

> Competitive work environments characterized by systematic programs of teacher evaluation and inservice training increase the abilities of teachers to teach.

OR

Collaborative work environments characterized by opportunities for individual and collective learning designed by the primary work groups increase the abilities of teachers to teach.

Most teacher evaluation procedures are designed to provide principals with the opportunity to clarify school goals and purposes with teachers, assess curricular and instructional decisions, observe classroom performance, and provide feedback on the quality of the teacher's performance. Discussions of teacher evaluation systems assert that their primary purpose is improvement; their structure is consistent with the belief that quality performance requires administrative supervision and feedback. These strategies implement the understanding of teacher work as technical skill, rather than professional expertise. They also are consistent with the assumption that motivation is external, rather than internal.

By contrast, collaborative work environments are sensitive to the complexities of professional decision making. The wide range of student needs can tax the expertise of any individual. Opportunities for collaboration bring the knowledge and abilities of a number of professionals to bear on decisions about learning activities for individual students. Meaningful collaboration replaces management control that conceals individual talents; collaboration among professionals provides the freedom to use those talents. Finally, collaboration reduces isolation. Thus professional decisions become public and accessible to the scrutiny and advice of colleagues.

This discussion of the supervision and evaluation of teachers serves as a reminder that "administrators are people, too." They vary, as do teachers, in their level of motivation. Nothing inherent in an administrative role guarantees high motivation. On the other hand, one has every reason to assume a Theory Y view of administrative behavior. The school administrator is just as likely to suffer the negative effects of an achievement-based, competitive testing environment as are teachers, probably more so if the district administrator believes that the buck stops — or should stop — in the principal's office.

Educational administrators should lay claim to professional status along with their teachers. Their roles are endlessly complex because of intensive demands of interaction with staff, students, parents, and supervisors. Administrators in schools and districts should use their own case to shape their view of others in the organization. Principals who are able to see themselves as metaphors for the other people in their schools will be able to increase their own contribution and that of others. Their sense of self-motivation will enable them to encourage self-motivation in others. Their own commitment to continued professional development will enable them to encourage professional development among teachers. They will sustain the same environment of cooperation, support, and nurturance for teachers that they want the central office to provide for them.

Contribution

People who participate in organized work are concerned about the quality of their products. In the case of schools, policy makers and the general public expect schools to deliver increased student achievement, decreased dropout rates, and other "outcomes." Parents want schools to care about their children and provide them with individualized opportunities to learn and develop. Students want schools that are responsive to their needs, that provide them with opportunities for social interaction; they want school people to care about them and to show them respect. Principals and teachers want to create learning environments that are safe and secure and foster academic achievement. They also want to create places that are good for adults, that provide collegial support and opportunities for professional development. All of these are important outcomes of educational organizations.

Means of Production and Initiators of Action

The next question is, How do principals, teachers, support staff, students, and community members contribute to the individual and collective achievement of all of these outcomes? Peters and Waterman's *In Search of Excellence* popularized the aphorism, "Productivity through people." Subsequently, the popular literature on organizational effectiveness adopted this orientation. Corporate executives, managers, politicians, and union leaders all voice agreement that people are the key to organizational success. However, what that means in practice depends on the underlying assumptions about the contributions of people to the work of the organization:

People are the means of production within the organization.

OR

59

People are the initiators of action and shapers of a work environment that fosters individual and collective achievement.

Barnard (1938) identified an important dilemma about the place of the individual in the organization:

> Sometimes in everyday work an individual is something absolutely unique, with a special history in every respect. This is usually the sense in which we regard ourselves, and so also our nearest relations, then our friends and associates. . . . The farther we push away from ourselves the less the word "individual" means what it means when applied to you and me. . . . (p. 12)

Barnard hit on a peculiar but well-documented human trait. People are quite generous in self-evaluation. In summarizing the research from business and industry, Lawler (1981) noted that individuals tend to overrate their own performance and underestimate the performance of others. Experience in and observation of individuals in the workplace verify that the farther away we move from ourselves, the less confident we are in the ability, commitment, energy, and good will of people.

Assumptions underlying organizational forms reinforce assumptions about the contribution of people in the workplace. Traditional bureaucratic organizations do not take a chance on people. An up-tight, orderly work environment is promoted through the hierarchy of authority, job specifications, an impersonal orientation toward organizational participants, and rules, regulations, and standard operating procedures. Instead of dealing with the dilemmas natural to collective work, traditional structures solve the problem by taking the people out of the picture. The hierarchy of authority reflects the belief that people lack ability and initiative. Consequently, domination is accepted as a necessary feature of collective work, and people are viewed as instruments of organizational productivity.

This depersonalization not only results in treating people as cogs in the organizational machinery, over time it also convinces workers that they are unable to influence the direction and context of their own work. When the organization conveys the message that it does not depend on people in any significant way, disengagement is a sensible human response. When interactions occur within power relationships, distrust is a reasonable reaction. When work is standardized, no room exists for difference.

These bureaucratic mindsets characterize most schools. Work is organized so that teachers are replaceable parts; long- and short-term substitutes are handled smoothly. Under these conditions, limiting

60

teachers' responsibilities to face-to-face instruction works for both teachers and administrators. Teachers create their own worlds within the classroom and leave schoolwide purposes and directions to others.

Casting the contributions of individuals as "means of production" depersonalizes and deskills the work environment. Viewing people merely as means to organizational ends protects the organization from variations among its workers, quiets dissenting voices, and flattens affective responses to organizational purposes and directions. But the cost to the organization is high, because it loses creativity and ingenuity; and the individual loses opportunities for commitment and connection to others with a common purpose.

The counter-assumption recognizes that people in organizations socially construct the meaning of their work, including conditions for success. Talented, self-directed, professionally committed individuals do not view their contributions as implementation of work routines. They view contribution in terms of participating in the design, enactment, and outcomes of their efforts and those of their colleagues. However, the principles of bureaucracy are so persistent and pervasive that most people have limited experience working within alternative structures built on principles of community, democracy, or social justice. Unfortunately, current efforts to increase participation through shared decision making or representative governance frequently are implemented within the boundaries of a bureaucratic framework.

Conclusion

The negative effects of conventional assumptions about people in the workplace link to principles of bureaucracy and hierarchy in ways that reinforce patterns of domination evident in the larger society. The impersonality of the bureaucratic structure promotes the artificial separation of public and private spheres. The domination of the hierarchy more than mirrors the domination of women and people of color in the larger society; it rationalizes domination in the name of efficiency and effectiveness. Treating people as the means of production strips them of their individuality, including their ability to make unique contributions to the organization. These reinforcing patterns of assumptions and structure make doubly difficult the eradication of racism, sexism, and ageism in day-to-day school operations. Democratic structures are more likely to support adult working relationships built on mutual respect and interdependence. Schools fit for human beings recognize that the greatest contributions of individuals are their abilities, commitment, and sense of responsibility toward their work.

CHAPTER FIVE

ASSUMPTIONS ABOUT SCHOOL PROCESSES

Assumptions about the work of schools are so strong that the processes of schooling look very much the same in thousands of schools across the country. Teaching and learning occur, for the most part, in age- and grade-level groupings within relatively isolated classrooms. Teachers are assigned to grade levels in the elementary school and to subject areas in the secondary school; instructional specialists are added to handle special students and curricula. The general curriculum is regulated by state and local policy makers, constrained by the availability of curricular materials, and adapted to fit the organizational context of the school and beliefs about students and learning. Instructional strategies conform to organizational contexts and curricular requirements.

Some school routines reflect decisions about practical ways of delivering instruction to large numbers of students. Some are based on principles of child and adolescent growth and development. Some are grounded in the work of teachers; others reveal attitudes toward students and decisions about their academic needs and potential. All of these ways of thinking affect decisions about which processes are viewed as effective, relevant, or practicable. Assumptions and counter-assumptions about the organizational and educational processes of schools cluster around three major dimensions: 1) organizing for teaching and learning; 2) planning and decision making; and 3) reviewing, reflecting, and reporting.

Organizing for Teaching and Learning

Contemporary school forms and practices have their roots in the early decades of this century. Compulsory attendance, immigration, and industrialization contributed to increased numbers of students. At the same time, the principles of scientific management pervaded business and industry. Growth, efficiency, and production were the order of the day. Not surprisingly, school boards, administrators, researchers, and professional associations all supported increased specialization and management innovations. Decisions about the design and operation of schools reflected then-popular beliefs about economies of scale. Choices about organizational form were intended to ensure the expeditious movement of large numbers of individuals, teachers and students, through a large number of tasks. Control was a major consideration, and schools adopted bureaucracy as an organizing pattern. However, principles of bureaucracy are inhospitable to principles of growth, development, teaching, and learning.

Efficiency and Flexibility

The competing perspectives are captured in traditional and counter-assumptions about the appropriate criteria for organizing and supporting teaching and learning:

> Assignment of teachers and students reflects organizational needs for operational efficiency and classroom needs for instructional simplicity.

OR

> Assignment of teachers and students reflects organizational needs for operational flexibility and classroom needs for instructional complexity.

Teaching and learning are dynamic, interactive processes. Consequently, the bases for teacher assignments to grade levels or subject areas are particularly important. Decisions are guided by several factors, such as overall staffing needs of the school, local budgets, state requirements for teacher certification, and union contracts. The image that prevails is one of teachers being assigned to classes on the basis of credentials and school needs. Students are assigned to classes on the basis of age, grade, level of ability, and interests.

However, the reality of assigning teachers and students to classes does not match these rational notions. Shortages of teachers in critical areas often result in the available teachers being assigned to work outside their areas of certification, training, and expertise. Senior teachers often are able to construct their work according to their preferences, while newer teachers are assigned to the least-desirable schools and classes. Hiring practices, especially in the large urban districts, are governed by policies on the reassignment of teachers and staffing based on student enrollment. Consequently, decisions to hire new teachers are delayed until after the school year has begun and enrollment has stabilized.

Student assignments are equally problematic. Oakes, Gamoran, and Page (1992) demonstrated that decisions about student grouping and class assignments are imbedded in beliefs about the broader school context, including:

- Beliefs about students' needs and abilities, the purpose of schooling, and a broad consensus about what school practices best accommodate these factors.
- Alternative clusters of knowledge and skills, emphases, or modes of presentation in subject areas, such as courses of study identified as college preparatory or vocational and reading programs divided into "levels" that vary in quantity and type of content.
- Criteria for determining the appropriate curricula for particular students, including ability, prior achievement, student or parent preferences, and completion of prerequisites.
- A process whereby students are identified as needing a particular curriculum based on teacher judgment, counselor guidance, survey of grades and test scores, student requests, or a combination of these factors.
- An organizational structure that allows the delivery of alternative curricula to different students, by means of within-class grouping, intact "grouped" classes, tracks, or other devices (pp. 570-571).

Discussions about grouping students for instruction are often contentious; the alternatives present practical problems. For instance, compelling evidence supports the heterogeneous grouping of girls and boys with diverse backgrounds, strengths, and talents. Yet, in practice, teachers are more likely to interact with highly verbal, task-oriented students who share their middle-class values. The 1992 report of the American Association of University Women, *How Schools Shortchange Girls*, provided ample evidence of the many ways in which schools fail to provide satisfactory learning opportunities for girls. Conversations among professional staff about the classes and assignments occur so rarely that difficulties and inequities, for both students and teachers, are seldom revealed. With few exceptions, teachers are out of the decision-making loop; thus tracking and categorizing students seem natural, and the categories feel real.

Arguably, grouping decisions are made on the basis of professionally determined individual needs and educational soundness. However, in the daily reality of schools, it is impossible to separate the ethical, pedagogical, and social justice dimensions of the decisions about whom to teach what:

> With tracking, educators prejudge how much children will benefit, with the result that some children are not taught knowledge that provides access to future academic and social opportunity. Those who see tracking as unfair do so largely because their assessment of the empirical evidence about tracking's outcomes is that "it doesn't work" — i.e., that tracking and rigid ability grouping are generally ineffective means for addressing individual differences and, for many children, harmful. (Oakes, Gamoran, and Page 1992, p. 596)

Proposed alternatives to rigid grouping practices are found primarily at the elementary school level. One is heterogeneous grouping of students accompanied by the implementation of cooperative learning strategies. Another is implied by the "regular education initiative," the inclusion of students with severe disabilities in regular classes. Whatever the benefits or drawbacks of these alternatives, they accept dominant assumptions about how schools should be organized and how the work of teachers should be defined. Organizational designs that isolate the work of teachers and students and limit the life space of teaching and learning promote simplicity and regularity at the expense of complexity and flexibility. Alternative assumptions offer a basis for making decisions about the organization of instruction on the principles of teaching, learning, human growth, and development. A relatively widespread contemporary example of such an alternative is found in middle schools in which heterogeneous groups of students work across subject areas with an interdisciplinary team of teachers.

Teachers need time to work through instructional activities with students. Rosenshine and Stevens (1986) developed a list of primary instructional functions of teachers that included: 1) reviewing previous day's work and reteaching, if necessary; 2) presenting new content; 3) guiding practice; 4) providing feedback; 5) organizing opportunities for independent practice; and 6) assessing student progress on a weekly or monthly basis. Of course, a list of functions misses the complex weaving of instructional strategies drawn from a broad repertoire of pedagogical skills, such as opportunities for active learning, cooperative learning, and teacher-directed instruction. And such a list misses the complexities of the classroom context that Doyle (1992), Fullan (1991), and others characterize by the following terms:

- Multidimensionality: many things happen.
- Simultaneity: many things happen at once.
- Immediacy: many things happen quickly.
- Unpredictability: unexpected things happen.
- Publicness: many students witness many of the things teachers do.
- History: things happen over time, leading to patterns of activities and behavior.

Johnson (1990) described the implications of the realities of classrooms and schools for teachers' work:

> A review of these features of school organizations — the environment, goals, technology, and raw materials — suggests that, if schools are to be effective, they must have adaptive structures, experiment with varied approaches, and prepare for different kinds of outcomes. Theory would lead us to predict that standardized structures and preplanned practices would enable educators to serve only some students and achieve only some goals, that rationalizing instruction overall would be ill-advised and ineffective. (p. 110)

Organizational processes of schools that are consistent with the demands of teaching and the needs of students are flexible and embody professional practices that are characterized by variety and responsiveness to diversity.

Curricular Commonality and Diversity

The contextual features of schools and classrooms and the instructional functions of teachers are related to decisions about what is taught. Assumptions about the curriculum reflect different perspectives:

> Curriculum is constructed around a common core of knowledge that reflects a common cultural heritage.

OR

> Curriculum is constructed around diverse knowledge that reflects a pluralistic cultural heritage.

The organization and political context of schools affect curricular decisions. Curriculum content is constantly debated, yet decisions about what to teach have remained relatively stable. Recent reform recommendations provide ample evidence of this stability. *A Nation at*

Risk (1983) identified the "new basics" that should be the focus of the curricular content: reading, writing, arithmetic, science, and computer use. The national educational goals specify that by the year 2000, students will graduate from high school with demonstrated competence in English, mathematics, science, history, and geography. A number of state education agencies have begun initiatives to design and implement a common core of learning. National and state testing programs operationalize the consensus about what should be taught, and curricular alignment matches the instructional focus to the content of the tests.

However, this apparent stability co-exists with substantial variability in what actually is taught. Curriculum is multi-dimensional and clearly more than merely a course of study. Jackson (1992, pp. 4-9) demonstrated that the "curriculum" includes:

- The *official* curriculum: the content of the course of study contained in state mandates, local curricular policy, and decisions about textbook adoption.
- The *unintended* curriculum: the "hidden" or unwritten understandings systematically communicated to students about accepted values, norms, and behaviors.
- The *unaccomplished* curriculum: the content or knowledge that was promised or is part of the official curriculum but was omitted because of teacher preferences or because time ran out.
- The *null* curriculum: "those course offerings or experiences that were not offered, making it, in effect, the curriculum that might have been."
- The *received* curriculum: the knowledge and content that actually engaged the students and that they learned.

The broadest definition of curriculum incorporates the full range of learning experiences provided to students and includes official, enacted, and received dimensions. Reflecting on educational practice and curricular policy underscores the fact that all of these dimensions, as they are currently implemented, are especially problematic for poor children, children of color, and girls.

The official curriculum incorporates majority perspectives about what is important and is oblivious to the lives and experiences of non-majority children and youth. Knowledge acquired in non-Western, non-white cultures often is relegated to special topics. To the extent that it represents majority culture, the official curriculum "whites out" knowledge and puts a decidedly masculine, middle-class, market-place spin on the content of instruction.

The enacted curriculum reflects decisions and organizational realities at the school and classroom levels. The structure of the secondary school day, which parcels curricular content and learning into six or seven 45- to 50-minute periods, artificially segments knowledge and blocks teachers from working through learning activities that may be sensitive to the needs and interests of the students. On the other hand, the elementary school schedule that groups children (heterogeneously or homogeneously) with one teacher operationalizes a belief that one person has all the skills and knowledge necessary to interact with any student and to respond to any need. In those instances in which the institution recognizes that this is not the case, specialists (in reading, music, special education, bilingual education, and so on) are provided; and students are pulled out of the "regular" class for specialized instruction.

The enacted curriculum also reflects beliefs about the kinds of conversations and subjects that belong in school. Although teaching, by its very nature, is highly personal and interactive, dominant assumptions about schooling and teaching erect barriers between teachers and students and cordon off academic content from the real experiences of learners and teachers. Fine (1991) provided provocative examples of the ways in which ideas and voices are silenced in school — and some hopeful examples of ways in which they are nurtured. Reflecting on her experiences, she summarized:

> Silencing provides a metaphor for the structural, ideological, and practical organization of comprehensive high schools. . . . Although the press for silencing is by no means complete or hermetic (that is, ripples of interruption, resistance, and outright rebellion are easy to spot), low-income schools officially contain rather than explore social and economic contradictions, condone rather than critique prevailing social and economic inequities, and usher children and adolescents into ideologies and ways of interpreting social evidence that legitimate rather than challenge conditions of inequity. (p. 61)

Alternative assumptions contextualize curriculum and instruction. Doyle noted:

> In recent years a growing number of scholars have challenged the production system conception of education and the technical rationality that underlies the professionalizing and scientizing of schooling. In particular, these scholars reject the fractionization of curriculum and pedagogy that seems inherent in these perspectives, as well as the practice of defining curriculum and teaching

practice out of context. . . . They argue that the curriculum exists not as a document but as a set of enacted events in which teachers and students jointly negotiate content and meaning. . . . Similarly, pedagogy is seen not simply as a neutral pipeline for delivering content, but as a social context that has fundamental curricular effects. (1992, p. 492)

High levels of interaction among teachers and students about learning activities foster curricular relevance, authenticity, and meaning. Students become disinterested in school when they are unable to see clear connections between what they learn and what they experience outside school (William T. Grant Foundation 1988). The curriculum needs to include different types of people, realistic settings, and ideas, values, beliefs, and perspectives that are alive with meaning for students. Curricular content lacks credibility and salience when it is not inclusive, honest, and thoughtful in dealing with societal issues. Doyle (1992) spells out the implications for teaching and learning:

> Teachers 'author' curriculum events to achieve one or more effects on students. In this sense, teachers are like other authors except that they are present while their works are being read. Teachers can therefore frame their works during enactment in classroom situations by guiding students through the texts, shaping the interpretations that are allowed on the floor, and, importantly, by creating tasks that students are to accomplish with respect to these texts. At the same time, students contribute to the authoring of curriculum events as they participate in these enactments. . . . The authoring of curriculum events is, therefore, a dynamic process in which content is produced and transformed continuously. (p. 508)

Routinization and Personalization of the School Day

Teachers and students bring to school a wide range of talents, interests, concerns, and problems. The type of personal interactions that occur over time affect the quality of individual relationships. Assumptions about the instructional context of the school and the classroom reflect beliefs about relationships between teachers and students.

> The life space for teaching and learning fits the time allocations and the daily routines imposed on teachers and students.

OR

70

> The life space for teaching and learning fits the demands of personal, interactive relationships between teachers and students.

Educational research documents many conditions that support learning. Students have positive school experiences when they: 1) achieve academic success (Natriello, McDill, & Pallas 1990); 2) develop positive social relationships in school (Lightfoot 1983; Sizer 1984); 3) perceive school to be relevant to their lives outside of school (Fine 1987); and 4) receive out-of-school support for their school participation (William T. Grant Foundation 1988). Yet the school day is not designed for the explicit purpose of maximizing the life space for teaching and learning. To the contrary, most designs seem to diminish such opportunities.

Student engagement with school requires connections with people in schools. Teachers are of prime importance. Children and youth need to know that adults care about them. In fact, students who drop out of school often report that no one cared (Fine 1987). Evidence from the New York City Dropout Prevention Project indicated that the students connected more with teachers in career education classes because the classes were more personalized and less formalized than academic classes (Grannis et al. 1988). A level of individual care and concern that is important to students requires sustained, in-depth social contact with teachers.

Opportunities for social contact with peers are also important. Sizer (1984) observed that, particularly for adolescents, the most important aspect of school is the opportunity to meet with friends. Schools that are sensitive to student needs provide opportunities for positive peer relationships through flexible schedules, access to extracurricular programs, interactive learning experiences, and school norms that support the development of caring, responsible peer associations.

The social aspects of schools are restricted in favor of organizational concerns about order and efficiency. No one would argue against the need for order and routine in schools. On the contrary, adults and children alike need assurance that their days will be characterized by some degree of certainty and predictability. However, traditional operating procedures often regularize the school day at the expense of teaching, learning, relationship building, and community. More flexible structures are needed to allow teachers to be responsive to the learning needs of all children. Arbitrary time limitations, class assignments, and credit hours interfere with the rhythm of teaching and learning and reduce opportunities for more personal connections between teachers and students.

Planning and Decision Making

The need for organizations to make mid-course corrections in their work, to respond to new demands, and to adapt to changing environments establishes the importance of planning and decision-making routines.

Rational and Participatory Planning

Different perspectives on planning are represented by competing assumptions:

> Planning is a management function that employs rational processes and formal techniques to project courses of action toward a desired future state for the organization.

> ### OR

> Planning is a participatory organizational process that involves teachers, parents, students, and administrators in discussing, imagining, and debating desirable alternative states for the immediate and long-term future.

An entire technology has grown up around the planning process. Computerized information systems are designed to maintain massive amounts of information about the people, work, and outcomes of the organization. Sophisticated systems try to organize mounds of operational data into usable information. Strategic planning systems collect information about the organizational, social, and political contexts using environmental scanning strategies.

These examples of the most popular contemporary planning tools are consistent with traditional organizational structures. More critically, they reinforce decision making that is distant from the core of the organization's work. The systems are so complex, specialized, and labor-intensive that planning professionals, whether outside consultants or in-house specialists, must be employed specifically to work through the planning process. No one with a job close to the organization's primary work can afford to spend the kind of time necessary for this function. Consequently, plans are developed elsewhere, and recommendations are merely reported to administrators. The only process remaining for teachers, parents, and administrators is political: mobilizing for or against the recommendations. The recommendations themselves are synthetic; they represent decontextualized perspectives that often have little meaning or relevance for the organizational participants.

At the same time, practical and necessary planning processes are subverted. Neither high school nor elementary teachers can spend even one uninterrupted hour each day to review student work and plan learning activities. Time for professional planning at the micro-level is extremely important to reflective practice and to the critique and improvement of education. With some exceptions in middle schools and alternative schools, time is not regularly available for teams or work groups of teachers to discuss student progress, develop curricular alternatives, or design instructional strategies.

Traditional planning is based on a narrow view that focuses on the identification of a preferred future state through rational processes. It reinforces and is reinforced by principles of authority and job specification. Alternatives view planning as lively, ongoing, inclusive processes. For example, plans take many forms:

- retrospective and introspective descriptions of the organization's work;
- communication devices for advertising what the organization is about;
- scenarios to debate and critique the work and directions of the organization;
- tentative maps of where people in the organization see themselves going; and
- opportunities to engage in thoughtful, provocative conversations with large numbers of participants and stakeholders in the organization (Clark 1981).

Centralized and Decentralized Decision Making

Decision-making processes are equally troubling. Teacher empowerment, shared decision making, and site-based management are popular contemporary reforms intended, first, to move the site of decision making from centralized sources closer to the work activity and, second, to broaden the scope of involvement in decision making to include more stakeholders. Implementation of these initiatives demonstrates the ways in which assumptions about decision making affect practice. Consider these competing assumptions:

73

Decision processes require administrators to seek advice from professional staff and others, develop consensus, and select options consistent with the school's goals, purposes, and processes.

OR

Decision processes require professional staff to identify and select a range of alternative options consistent with principles of teaching and learning and the value referents on which the school community is based.

Efforts by school administrators to introduce more inclusive, action-based decision processes have been plagued by problems of implementation. Those problems are rooted in continued acceptance of the assumption that decision making ultimately is an administrative responsibility. Shared decision-making initiatives that retain administrative control do not enlarge the scope of decision making or empower teachers and parents to make more decisions. This is a change of form, not substance.

Decision making in schools is concerned with more than operational and management decisions; it involves choices about the substantive work of the school, based on the interests of the school community. However, when decision-making authority is considered a managerial function, the decisions remain narrowly focused on management issues and concerns. Some of these are close to the technical core and are important to teachers, such as student and teacher assignments or student discipline practices. Others may be important to the management of the school but are remote from the technical core and thus within the teachers' zone of indifference, such as requisition procedures.

Teachers make scores of decisions every day in the privacy of their classrooms. Decision-making processes with real meaning for the work of schools would engage professional staff and others, including parents and students. Currently, the formal decisions that are made in schools are primarily administrative. Consequently, a decision deficit exists at the level of the technical core. Alternatives would elevate the importance of the technical core and increase the number and types of options that might be considered.

Reviewing, Reflecting, and Reporting

Professional educators are concerned about the accountability of schools for their outcomes. Teachers and principals need to participate in processes that allow them to reflect on their work, analyze a wide range of information about its quality, and debate alternative courses of action. Since professional educators are public servants, they also have a responsibility to report on their work and its outcomes to key stakeholders.

Standardized and Collaborative Assessment

Student outcomes constitute a critical component of the work of schools. Strategies for identifying and evaluating student outcomes reflect competing assumptions about the assessment of student achievement:

> Standardized testing documents student achievement and informs decisions about students' programs of learning.

> **OR**

> Assessment is a collaborative effort between teachers and students to understand student learning and open possibilities for student growth.

The educational processes that make up the work of schools provide the context within which teachers, counselors, and administrators make decisions about students. The assignment of students to particular courses or teachers establishes the basis of the learning community for students. Counselors, administrators, and teachers decide on the learning opportunities that will be made available. Teachers decide what patterns of interaction will prevail in the classroom. Administrators decide what will happen to students who do not conform to school norms or regulations. All of these decisions affect the type of learning community that the students will experience.

Current reform strategies rely on standardized testing and assessment strategies as a basis for educational decisions. Testing experts assert their ability to develop instruments that are valid, reliable, and authentic measures of student achievement. Policy makers at the federal and state levels have made achievement tests the centerpiece of school improvement proposals. However, the unfairness of tests has long been argued:

> Though available evidence is largely indirect, it seems clear that these practices (using test scores to judge students' abilities and to group them into homogeneous ability groups or tracks) and attitudes (educators viewing test scores as the most accurate indi-

cator of student ability) have had a widespread impact in limiting the educational opportunities of minority students in American schools for most of the twentieth century. (Haney 1993, p. 65)

Experts in testing establish the merits of achievement tests through statistical tests of validity and reliability. However, Haney (1993) argued that psychometricians miss the low level of *educational* validity of tests in the nontechnical sense; that is, the extent to which the information provided by tests helps teachers educate children. In the interest of child growth and development:

> What needs to be opposed is the use of tests that serve to justify and perpetuate social and educational disadvantages of minorities. And from a more positive perspective, what is needed is to use test results not so much to make decisions about individual students, as to examine critically how schools are serving their interests. (p. 71)

Educational practice has been narrowed by an undue emphasis on standardized assessment of student achievement. Alternative perspectives view assessment quite differently. Instead of relying on standardized tests to make decisions about schooling, assessment is seen as a collaborative, interactive process between teachers and students, which is a regular component of learning activities. Students are engaged in discussions and decision making that empower them to participate in their own learning. They develop descriptions of what they understand and how they came to understand it. "Objective" tests, designed outside the classroom, are replaced by the ongoing processes within the classroom to understand students' learning, build on students' strengths, and modify instructional practices. Collaboration between teachers and students in assessing learning is extremely important:

> As teachers and students define "schoolwork" with and for one another, setting the limits and enlarging the possibilities for success in their joint endeavor, they jointly construct the meaning of commitment and engagement. The "bargains" and "treaties" struck between students and teachers both reflect and reproduce the expectations that each group holds for the other's performance. (Little 1990, p. 193)

Measuring Standards and Improving Processes

Scores on standardized achievement tests provide very limited information about the achievements, growth, and development of students. Whether they are seen as providing useful, credible information about the quality of the school depends on the competing assumptions about school effectiveness:

> The quality of the school's work is determined by measuring the extent to which it promotes achievement on standardized tests.

OR

> The quality of the school's work is determined by regularized assessments of educational processes, professional practices, and student outcomes by professional staff, students, parents, and other stakeholders.

The purpose of accountability mechanisms is to provide the tools and processes through which organizational participants make sense of what they do and clients receive information about the quality of the work in which they have a stake. Policy makers have placed their confidence in setting standards of student achievement and comparing schools and districts on the extent to which they meet those standards. This strategy is reinforced by assumptions about the necessity of competition for improvement and the belief that controlling outcome measures will serve as an impetus to school change.

However, performance standards fail on at least three grounds. First, local school administrators and school boards complain that they are not playing on an even field. Schools and districts vary in terms of their funding, the socioeconomic status of the local population, and the variety of needs that children bring to school. As a result, state policy makers have adopted complicated groupings of school districts on the basis of economic and school context variables. Comparisons then occur within a "look-alike" group. On the surface, these comparisons seems fair. However, these practices institutionalize expectations of limited success in teaching children from low-income households.

Second, the performance measures most often consist of achievement tests with performance standards that represent expected levels of knowledge and skill acquisition. Performance measures and standards, then, create the substantive focus of the educational experience for teachers and students. Local schools are able to adjust their practices only at the technical level. Schools may be free to respond to local needs, but that response must occur within the boundaries established by non-local authorities. That is the intent of state policies about systemic reform and federal policies that establish national tests and national standards.

Finally, performance standards and measures ignore the qualities of schools that are critical to establishing vibrant learning communities of difference. The preferred outcomes are narrowly defined around acquisition of knowledge segments. But more aspects of the school experience contribute to making a high-quality school. What are the relationships between teachers and students? Does the school environment support ongoing professional learning and opportunities for intense professional engagement? How do the interactions in and outside the classroom promote tolerance and appreciation of diversity and encourage meaningful learning for all children, regardless of gender, race, ethnicity, or disabling condition? Is the curriculum authentic, relevant, and representative of the multicultural dimensions of a pluralistic society? How are democratic principles of social justice implemented in the organization of the school? These are vital questions for local educators, parents, and students; but they are missing from policies that hold schools accountable for predetermined standards of student performance.

An alternative perspective focuses on critical analysis of professional practice. Accountability mechanisms provide opportunities for teachers, administrators, students, parents, and other stakeholders to assess the quality of professional practice and the multiple outcomes of schools. Time and space are made in school routines for discussions about the quality of learning activities and the character of the school community. Administrators use a full array of resources to provide information to teachers that they can use to assess the quality of education. Evaluation of educational practice moves substantially beyond symbolic standards to the improvement of processes that have meaning for all the stakeholders.

No one argues against the importance of school people being held accountable for their professional practice. The problem is that the most popular, contemporary accountability mechanisms are narrow, naive, and divorced from the complexities of practice. Alternatives build assessment into all of the critical dimensions of education in ways that are broad, sophisticated, and connected to the real problems and demands of professional practice.

Conclusion

School processes represent educational practice at the micro-level. Assumptions about the organizational and educational processes of schools are linked to form a coherent set of professional practices. The

78

dimensions of learning and the character of the learning community reflect beliefs about the work of teachers, the content of the curriculum, and opportunities for reflection and improvement. To the extent that the assignment of teachers is based on principles of organizational efficiency, professional practice is isolated; teachers' interest, understanding, and participation in the full life of the school are limited; and the possibility of establishing meaningful, working relationships with students is hindered. To the extent that the substantive work of the school is reduced to predetermined standards of student achievement, decision options about student learning are narrowed, responsiveness to local needs and interests is impeded, the relevance of school to diverse populations of students is blocked, and students and professional staff are marginalized and their voices silenced.

Alternative assumptions underscore authentic reform. When the work of teachers is grounded in principles of teaching and learning, strategies are developed to enhance their participation in decision making and planning, deepen their relationships with students, and bring their diverse talents and skills to bear on the improvement of professional practice. When curriculum is seen as including comprehensive opportunities for learning, attention is drawn to the excitement of academic pursuits that reflect the diversity of a pluralistic society; the stinging persistence of racism, sexism, ageism, and classism in society; and the hope connected to learning communities of difference built on principles of social justice and responsibility.

School processes also are imbedded in larger social, political, and organizational contexts and are affected by the assumptions that dominate them. For example, meritocratic views of schooling reinforce externally driven performance standards and the competitive environments they create. Beliefs about a common cultural heritage narrow the range of knowledge, events, and understanding considered important enough to be included in the school curriculum. An assumption about the necessity of bureaucracy establishes a hierarchy that reduces the authority of professional educators to make decisions, narrows the work of teachers, and decreases emphasis on professional expertise.

The assumptions that dominate thinking about school processes limit the identification of alternatives that can open possibilities for improvement. The nesting of assumptions across political, social, structural, and individual contexts creates beliefs about professional practice in schools that are strong deterrents to organizational renewal.

CHAPTER SIX

EXPANDING THE POSSIBILITIES FOR AUTHENTIC EDUCATION REFORM

Do the current dominant assumptions about education reform make authentic reform impossible? Not unless we continue to treat them as if they are aphoristic and exclusionary. They surely are not aphoristic; and to the extent that they are tolerated as exclusive, they will wreak further penalties on the already disadvantaged.

At the beginning of this book we asked a question that we now wish to revisit: What sort of reform is this, anyway? Now it is time to redefine the question with more precision:

- For whom are the benefits of education reform intended?
- Who are the reformers and where will the reform occur?
- What role could or should be played by government functionaries, academics, and advocates for reform, some of whom now believe they are the agents of reform?

Beneficiaries of Reform

All of us can benefit from a more effective education system. Periodically, groups encouraging higher expenditures for education point out the cost savings to be realized by investing in education now, rather than in welfare or incarceration later; the instrumental value of education to economic growth and competitiveness for American business; or the reduced health costs associated with a better educated population.

However, all of these legitimate contentions beg the question. The benefit of education reform is to and for our children — one by one. At issue is the entitlement of each child to life, liberty, and the pursuit of happiness. That right cannot be realized unless each child has a successful elementary and secondary school experience. Failure in school can be compensated for only by privilege of wealth or family. The child whose family is not influential or economically advantaged is doomed to an adulthood of poverty, disease, and early death with a certainty almost as high as if he or she were condemned by public decree.

The issue of each child, not children collectively, needs emphasis. To obtain an affective as well as a cognitive response to this claim for entitlement, reformers need to have a real individual in mind. What child, what son or daughter, what neighbor's youngster comes to mind? That is the individual for whom the entitlement is claimed. What happens to this child when she or he is unfairly assigned to a "slow" group or is held back a grade and then sits in a classroom desperate to know what's going on but hopelessly behind? What happens when no adult in the school knows or cares enough about this child to do other than write him or her off as hopeless?

What happens to this child in high school: absent most days, on the street, in contact with drugs and a criminal subculture. Will this youngster still struggle to finish high school, particularly in a state or school district that requires an examination that this youth knows he or she cannot pass? But that state or district will not spend enough time or money for tutorial assistance to prevent this failure. Then imagine that you, personally, cannot intervene. You have only enough money to provide survival subsistence. You have no skill in accessing the school. You can only stand by and watch your daughter or son be crippled by circumstance and cut off from any reasonable chance as an adult.

Try to picture your reaction to some of the current reform proposals. Let's put money into preschool education where recidivism will be less and the return on the dollar will be higher (but your son is 13 years old). Let's create a Tech Prep track that is comparable to college prep so these youngsters are at least employable (but your daughter is gifted, capable of college with a little help). Let's raise standards for graduation or insert a standardized test in grade 11 or 12 so that employers are guaranteed a "quality" product (but your son or daughter is a quality person who never had enough academic help). And now let's print her academic record on her high school diploma so that no one who might hire her will be misled into thinking she will be a competent employee.

We have to stop thinking this way. Reform in education is for children and youth. In his last novel, *The Thanatos Syndrome,* Walker Percy's narrator reports the "secret belief" transmitted by Dr. Harry Stack Sullivan to a group of medical students who are making patient rounds with him:

Here's the secret. . . . You take that last patient we saw. Offhand, what would you say about him? A loser, right? A loser by all counts. You know what you're all thinking to yourself? You're thinking, No wonder that guy is depressed. He's entitled to be depressed. If I were he, I'd be depressed too. Right? Wrong. You're thinking the most we can do for him is make him feel a little better, give him a pill or two, a little pat or two. Right? Wrong. Here's the peculiar thing and I'll never understand why this is so: Each patient this side of psychosis, and even some psychotics, has the means of obtaining what he needs, she needs, with a little help from you. Incidentally, Doctors, How do we know you don't look like losers to me, or I to you? (p. 16)

The narrator continues:

But there it was, to me the pearl of great price, the treasure buried in a field, that is to say the patient's truest unique self which lies within his, the patient's, power to reach and which we, as little as we do, can help him reach.

Do you know that this is true? I don't know why or how, but it is true. People can get better, can come to themselves, . . . with a little help from you. (pp. 16-17)

Our children must not be losers. Our schools cannot give up on a single one. We have to believe that reform can be designed to provide them with "a little help," to allow them to reach their "truest unique self," and to "come to themselves" with a little help from schools. There can be no exclusions.

Authentic education reform will be demonstrated, not by exit examinations but by the number of "losers" who become "winners"; by the number of students who discover that their life holds the promise of choices; and by the opportunity these students realize to enjoy a fulfilling and productive adulthood. Anything less is unacceptable.

Reformers and the Locus of Reform

We define the problems and the solutions of school reform in local terms: one student, one parent, one teacher, one principal, one classroom, one school. If reform in education is to occur, the reformers will be the actors at the school level. One of the most successful of those actors, Deborah Meier, principal of Central Park East Secondary School in New York City, frames the rationale for bottom-up changes essentially as we view it (Meier 1992):

Education reformers, regardless of political persuasion, have too often [viewed] local school boards as irrelevant . . . and thus [viewed] school reform as a task best accomplished by national policy-makers.

The irony is that schools in fact stand as one of the few remaining institutions that can easily be influenced at the community level. . . . The debate over education reforms belongs in local communities. Only such a community-centered debate will restore the public's sense that it has a stake in the public schools.

If America can commit itself to this task — educating all children well — the historic promise of free public schooling will be fulfilled. It doesn't require a nationalized curriculum backed by a high-stakes testing program that falsely promises order and control; or a privatized market driven system offering the illusion of freedom and individuality. What it requires is tough but doable: generous resources, thoughtful and steady work, respect for the diverse perspectives of the people who work in and attend our schools, and finally, sustained public interest in and tolerance for the process of reinvention. (p. 272)

The democratic process thrives under circumstances of high interest, knowledgeability, expertise, and commitment. Parents, concerned citizens, and a professional staff of teachers and administrators hold the potential to solve their own educational problems with a little help from auxiliary agents serving in supportive capacities in the state capitals, Washington, D.C., colleges and universities, regional educational laboratories, and research and development centers. No one cares more about students than the students themselves and their parents. No one is risking more in the process of education than these actors. No one knows more about individual schools and classrooms than the schools' professional staff. Local communities need their schools; and they need an interactive role with schools to foster a sense of community, as well as to improve education.

There is no easy route to authentic reform in American schools. The real reformers are in the schools and communities of this country now. If they cannot be trusted to lead the reform, no amount of external mandates and controls will work. We need to find ways to support them, to encourage them, and to free them to be excellent.

Agents, Advocates, and Academics

Reform in American education can be, and in some cases is being, supported by non-local intermediaries. State-level executive and legislative officials have significant regulatory and financial obligations to fulfill. The less significant, constitutional role of the federal government allows it to concentrate on issues such as protection of human rights, categorical financial assistance, and exhortatory advocacy from the "bully pulpit." Individual reformers, support groups, advocates of particular reforms, academics, and bridging agencies all support the change process and stimulate the spread of new ideas that enrich the dialogue of reform.

However, the significance of these non-local roles has grown substantially over the past 10 to 15 years. Education in the United States is a state function; and state education agencies have adopted or established regulatory, stimulatory, supervisory, and supportive legislation to fulfill this function. The issue is not whether such roles are important to education (they obviously are) or whether they could be useful in education reform (they obviously could be). The issue is to place them in perspective. Governmental functionaries have special obligations to protect localities, schools, and ultimately students and parents from malfeasance and incompetence. They are required to act in the public interest, as the federal government has done in support of equity in education regardless of race, gender, or disabling condition. Many state legislatures and courts now are grappling with the vexatious issue of equity in the funding of schools. Individual reformers and reform agencies not only have proposed reforms, but in some instances have established national networks to foster the dissemination of their version of school reform.

Yet when schools open each fall, the actors are the professional and support staff and the students and their parents at the local school. When instruction begins, the interaction is between teachers and students. Real reform is in their hands, as it should be. External agents and agencies can intrude on the school — and more are attempting to do so. They can offer generic solutions to particularized problems — and they also are doing this. They can attempt to mandate, control, and engineer change. But, in the final analysis, their efforts must be secondary to what happens in local schools.

At the same time, external agents and agencies can take on some exciting roles in school reform. They can facilitate and support local reforms. They can offer encouragement and stimulation to local reformers. They can provide staff-development assistance and build communication links between local schools and other support agencies. Education reform is a complex process, not an event. It occurs over time, not at one time. Non-local participants in the process need to recognize who the reformers are, where the action is, and how they, as non-locals, can play effective, non-prescriptive roles in support of local school reformers.

The Essence of Reform

The current, dominant assumptions controlling education reform are a complex nest of beliefs, practices, political predispositions, actions, and compromises of expediency and advantage. Some are relatively new, but most of them are hoary. The very organization of schools is indebted to the link between school and industry, seen as a model of bureaucratic efficiency during the first decade of this century. A meritocratic view of schooling derives from a meritocratic view of American society. The standardized testing movement is three-quarters of a century old and is one of the earliest — and most durable — examples of the successful nationwide diffusion of an educational practice of the post-World War I era. The school as a melting pot for American society, often described as the common school, is the heritage of the earliest waves of immigration. The Horatio Alger myth, the low status of teaching, the sanitized curriculum of whiteness and maleness, the high school schedule, ability tracking, the inevitability of school failure and retention — all are practices and beliefs to which we have become accustomed.

More recent pernicious shifts in policies have increased the obstacles to school reform. From the 1980s to date, the day-to-day plight of poor families and their children has grown exponentially. The shifts from equity concerns to standards of performance, from access to selectivity, and from social concerns to economic concerns have introduced a new and threatening level of school failure for millions of students.

The route out of this miasma of educational failure will require educators and others to confront directly the assumptions that are at the root of the problem. We have tried to bring those assumptions to light in this book by introducing counter-assumptions. The dominant assumptions are powerful because they 1) have long historic roots, 2) are nested across domains of thought as broad as the social context of schooling and as narrow as educational processes, and 3) represent compromises that the powerful and affluent in our society have found acceptable.

In moral and ethical terms and, as our society is now discovering, even in terms of expediency, these dominant assumptions are wrong. The cost in human suffering and life is too high. They represent a

flawed belief system and cannot serve as an adequate basis for education reform.

In the next few pages we will revisit the assumptions within broad
categories that we feel cluster the assumptions across domains into nine
critical choices for public policy about education. Our contention is
that moving from the dominant policy position to an alternative is imperative if we are to succeed in education reform. These are, in our
judgment, either-or propositions. They do not represent continua, but
choices. If one chooses a universalistic rather than a meritocratic focus
on achievement and success in school, it is not an argument against recognizing and rewarding individual initiative and achievement. However, it is a statement of commitment to organize and operate the school
and the entire program of child and family support so as to prepare all
children, every child, to share in the benefits of this society. The basic
purpose against which the school is measured changes in terms of its
orientation to the client. A student's failure becomes the organization's
failure.

Following sections will briefly examine basic shifts in beliefs, policies, and practices that are necessary to move ahead with authentic
reform:

- from individual to institutional responsibility for achievement;
- from instrumentality to entitlement;
- from control to empowerment;
- from the inevitability to the interruptability of outcomes;
- from bureaucracy to democracy;
- from commonality to diversity;
- from interconnected services to open, comprehensive child and
  family services;
- from competition to collaboration;
- from intervention to facilitation.

From Individual to Institutional Responsibility for Achievement

The political assertions — 1) that schools need only to provide a
conducive environment in order for children to progress on the basis of
their own ability and 2) that achievement in school is predominantly
controlled by the student — seem, on their face, to be a cynical interpretation of a fair chance. Prior to entering school, and on a continuing
basis throughout the years of schooling, a high percentage of youth
confront poverty and disadvantaging conditions in their non-school
lives. To support the argument that individuals can "go it alone," one

needs to assume that schools can effect only marginal gains in the education of students or that internal structures such as competition, high standards, and high-stakes assessment will compensate for the disadvantage.

The individual in control of his or her achievement seems possible, although not optimum, for gifted students or even for above-average students from economically secure homes. However, the concept of individual control over achievement, given the limited available tools to support it — high standards, competition, and comparative assessment — is antithetical to school success for large numbers of students. Such a concept depresses academic achievement for all but the most talented students.

From Instrumentality to Entitlement

The attraction of instrumentalism as the test of an educational system's success is undeniable. Who does not want economic prosperity and social stability? The organization of America's workplace in the industrial era utilized a bureaucratic structure that viewed people as the means of production. The interest that business and industry took in education during the 1980s reform movement reflected the necessity of a well-trained work force to support international competitiveness. And from the student's viewpoint, especially those not going on to college, is it not of prime importance to them to be employable and self-supporting?

There is another viewpoint to be expressed in regard to linking education to the instrumental needs of society. Many persons — the majority of those who, increasingly, live in poverty-stricken metropolitan and rural areas — are not excited about maintaining their disadvantaged place in American society through their children. American workers are not thrilled at being viewed as "means of production." Training for the workplace in secondary schools often means giving up, at age 13 or 14, the chance of meeting minimal requirements to attend a state-supported university.

But a fundamental reason to eschew instrumentality is a simple belief in the right of all American children to life, liberty, and the pursuit of happiness. Education's first responsibilities are to ensure the entitlement of the young to the best that society has to offer and to serve as an agent of societal improvement and transformation. Instrumentality dooms not just children but all of society to be no better than it is.

From Control to Empowerment

Trust and power are the critical perspectives on people and institutions that reinforce conditions and mechanisms of control. An assumption of many in the political arena is that the public schools lack the strength and vitality to transform themselves into healthy, relevant societal institutions. This assumption is strengthened by beliefs that school people — teachers, principals, students, parents — left to themselves, will not have the sense of responsibility and the drive to excel at work and learning. Both of these beliefs are buttressed by bureaucratic structures and processes that take decision making out of the hands of people in schools and constrain their actions through external systems of standards and evaluation. The result is a reined-in, up-tight public school system that immobilizes action and renewal.

The root of externally dominated reform rests in the low status accorded educators in this country. From the effort to produce teacher-proof mathematics and science curricula in the early days of the Course Content Improvement Program of the National Science Foundation to the current emphasis on rigidly programmed outcome-based education curricula, curriculum alignment with testing systems, and curriculum mapping devices, the image of the teacher as technician is clear. However, it would be difficult to imagine an enterprise that, on its face, has a more able, better educated work force than American public schools. Today's teachers universally hold baccalaureate degrees, and many have advanced training. When parents rate their children's teachers in national polls, they express high levels of confidence in their abilities.

Authentic education reform cannot have it both ways. The vital reformers are and will be the teachers and administrators at the local school level. They are the ones who work day-in and day-out with children. They are the ones who daily face a wide array of professional decisions. Technical skills are insufficient to handle the responsibilities of teaching. Classroom complexities require increasingly higher levels of professional expertise. If there are serious problems with the professional abilities of teachers and administrators, the solution lies in improving the preparation and inservice training of educators, not in attempting to convert teaching into a technical activity.

The hope of authentic reform rests in empowerment that generates action at the site of responsibility by encouraging people to assume responsibility for themselves. When self-control replaces bureaucratic control, people are free to work at the edge of their competence and, consequently, to develop in ways that expand the limits of their expertise.

From Inevitability to Interruptability of Outcomes

Reform efforts are unlikely to flourish under conditions of despair. Negative factors that decelerate reform include assumptions about the lack of viability of American public schools, the uselessness of further investment in the schools, and the acceptance of low socioeconomic status as a condition that dooms poor youngsters to school failure. The weakest link in contemporary schools has been an inability to interrupt the deterministic relationship of socioeconomic status and school performance. However, individual schools, classrooms, and teachers across the country demonstrate daily that the deterministic relationship can be interrupted.

The public schools have been caught in a negative cycle of hyperbole. Their failures have been exaggerated; their achievements unrecognized or diminished. Although public schools are modestly funded, they have been depicted as "fat cats." Most reform initiatives have been designed by policy makers remote from practice and mandated for those closest to practice. Day-to-day practitioners have been pushed into control-driven reforms that increase the difficulties that schools face when they try to respond to their least-able students. The time is past-due to recognize that most schools are working and can work better with a little help, encouragement, and trust. *All* schools can do what some schools are doing; they can interrupt the deterministic relationship between socioeconomic status and educational outcomes.

From Bureaucracy to Democracy

The strength of dominant assumptions about the need for bureaucracy is demonstrated by the persistence and pervasiveness of bureaucratic organizations. The structures, processes, and people in the bureaucratic workplace are wrapped tightly, which limits their movement, growth, and entrepreneurial activities. The nature of the work is specified, activities are held within predetermined limits, and individual responsibility is replaced by measures of institutional outcomes. Organizational accountability becomes a proxy for the growth and development of the professional staff and their students. The result is isolation and "rugged individualism" in the workplace, because the social and professional values that bind people together are supplanted by mechanical and technical procedures and goals that drive people apart.

Democracy, on the other hand, is rooted in beliefs about the efficacy of people and their ability to handle the responsibilities demanded of them in the social, political, and organizational contexts in which they work. Organizations and processes consistent with democracy replace domination with freedom, and individualism with collective obligation and trust. Organizing schools as communities of difference in a pluralistic society requires the invention of democratic mechanisms that promote individual rights within a cooperative environment of social responsibility.

From Commonality to Diversity

In some respects the move from an emphasis on commonality to diversity makes a virtue of a necessity. The ethnic demographics of the next 20 years are essentially a certainty. The number of white births is declining, while the number of Hispanic and African-American births is growing. About 70% of school children in 1990 were white; only about 50% will be white in 2020. While only one in nine youngsters in 1990 was Hispanic, that proportion will grow to one in four by 2020. Whatever advantage might have been asserted for schools to promote a so-called common cultural heritage seems not only Eurocentric but egocentric in today's increasingly diverse American society.

The argument in favor of abandoning this parochial view is not simply inevitability or defensiveness. The vitality of a culture and a country is enhanced by redefining and rediscovering its cultural self. This vitality comes about only through the process of understanding, appreciating, and incorporating the diverse cultural traditions of its people. The result is a society that is capable of improvement, growth, and transformation. Educationally, schools that adopt a curriculum constructed around a pluralistic cultural heritage are stronger and better able to relate to children who are currently outside the mainstream of society.

From Interconnected Services to Comprehensive Child and Family Services

Few policy makers cling to the belief that the school can succeed in its educational mission without continuing relationships with the community and with social, medical, nutritional, and welfare agencies. The current policy issues are: 1) whether community linkages are ancillary or integral to the school's operation, and 2) whether coordinated non-educational services can be provided across independent agencies through interorganizational arrangements or must be integrated in a new comprehensive agency.

If school reform is to go beyond minimal levels of academic success for students from poor households, it seems unlikely that either conventional school-home relationships or cooperative-contractual arrangements with social and welfare agencies can do the job. Interrupting the relationship between low socioeconomic status and limited academic success will require major adjustments in the school-community setting in order to provide intensive interventions that meet the physical, environmental, psychological, and educational needs of youngsters. Basic change in child and family support mechanisms will be needed; and success will be more likely in the context of a seamless relationship between the school, its community, and social and welfare agencies.

Interconnected services, of which the school is merely one service, are no longer sufficient. An integrated child and family support center is a better image. For all the reasons that bureaucracies find coordination across agencies difficult and ineffective, we believe that a comprehensive child and family support program within a single agency that focuses on improving the lives of children should be the goal of reformers. For all the reasons that conventional school-parent-community participation programs have failed to attract community involvement in schools, we believe that the school community should have a powerful voice in the operation of its school.

The delivery site may well turn out to be a school building that is transformed into a child and youth services center. The school's role as a community center will be fulfilled when the school is perceived to be a place in which the comprehensive needs of children and families come first. The school's central role in the community will be established when the members of the school community have a controlling interest in its operation and success.

From Competition to Collaboration

Competition is ingrained in the American psyche; thus it goes wholly unchallenged as a fundamental value. Competition connotes success against all odds, undaunting perseverance in the face of tribulation, the triumph of the individual, the "thrill of victory and the agony of defeat." It cuts across social, political, organizational, and individual dimensions of life as a necessary condition for success. Current education reforms reflect beliefs in individual responsibility and the necessity of competition as an incentive to personal as well as institutional achievement. Tests, standards, and monitoring systems built on comparisons of productivity across schools, districts, and states reinforce competition as the environment for improvement.

However, competition is a slogan, not a principle on which to build lives or effective organizations. The rhetoric of competition in education reform ignores the cooperative contexts in which competition often occurs. In sports, the most popular analogy, individual talent is coupled with teamwork. Valuable players are good teammates, as well as talented individuals. In the market place, success in the free-enterprise system is explained more by social, political, and organizational factors than by the creation of internal contests. And organizational analysts continue to assert the necessity of cooperation and collaboration in the context of a global economy.

Meaningful education reform is rooted in cooperative, collaborative action. Cooperation is a necessary condition for the interpersonal trust, support, and challenge that enhance opportunities for individual growth and institutional renewal. The societal context of schools, the explosion of knowledge, and the needs of children and youth are too complex for individuals to go it alone.

From Intervention to Facilitation

Currently, most popular reform initiatives place a high level of confidence in the efficacy of externally engineered interventions, such as setting standards, conducting assessments, formalizing power relationships, and establishing sanctions for failure. These initiatives fit the assumption that there is a general lack of confidence in the self-motivation of school people and thus a need to create and control work environments for teachers and students. A contrasting view of the process of reform, which is supported by empirical research on change in public and private organizations, emphasizes the role of change agents as facilitators, providers of resources, and consultants. In his comprehensive review of research on change in education, Fullan (1991) noted:

> Grappling with educational change in self-defeating ways has been the modal experience over the last 30 years. . . . The response of many has been to redouble their efforts. For those in authority this has meant more advocacy, more legislation, more accountability, more resources, etc. For those on the receiving end the response has been more closed doors, retreats into isolationism or out of education altogether, and in some cases, collective resis-

93

tance. We have seen that these seemingly rational political solutions, while perfectly understandable if one is in a hurry to bring about or avoid change, simply do not work. In fact, they do more harm than good as frustration, tension, and despair accumulate. (pp. 345-346)

However, adopting an alternative view of the change process that supports local initiative requires an attitude of confidence and trust in those required to change. It requires confidence in their professional competence, their commitment to effective education for all children, and their willingness to entertain new ways of doing things. As Fullan noted, it also requires the patience to tolerate decentralized change when mandated change holds at least the illusion of results "in a hurry."

Perhaps we need to turn the issue of change upside down. We know with reasonable certainty that imposed change by external agencies does not work well. These external agencies seem to be the first group from whom change is required. They must recognize that generic solutions will not fit local needs, that mandates provoke resistance, that significant change requires time for those who must change to test and modify appropriate solutions, and that those closest to the point of action normally know more about effective solutions to local problems than those remote from the point of action. If the change agents can modify their plans and behavior from the role of interveners to the role of facilitators, they can in turn create conditions of innovation and change in schools.

Alternative Policies for Reform

We would like to imagine that the lack of hope for authentic education reform in the 1980s has given way to a period of latency for authentic reform in the 1990s. What is there, beyond wishful thinking, that would suggest that this decade might entertain a broader range of reform policies? At a minimum, the current federal policy environment is kinder toward a broader, more diverse range of the citizenry. This political posture is more likely to tap into a broadly held predisposition in the country to worry about childhood, adolescence, and the less fortunate. This predisposition is exemplified more accurately in terms of those we know personally than in the current policies governing child and family support; but it provides a base from which to envision a more enlightened future.

The last few years have provided evidence that our present policies governing education reform are not working. They have not been discredited only because the blame for their failure has been shifted by the national and state reformers to "inadequate implementation" by "inept" local practitioners. Rationalizations of this sort eventually fall of their own weight. The current knowledge base, not just in the field of education but in the broader fields of study reviewed in this book, provides convincing evidence that the 1980s path to reform on which we continue to run will also continue to lead us astray. We're trying hard enough; we're just trying the wrong things. The alternative policies for education reform described in this chapter have been characterized in the past two decades as either "radical" or "soft." To the contrary, they are singly and collectively the practical and commonplace expressions of American communities, parents, and citizens:

- a strong desire to support our children;
- a commitment to give everyone a fair chance to succeed, and subsequent chances as long as they need them;
- a basic confidence in the efficacy of people, singly and in community groups, to handle their own affairs and improve matters at the local level;
- a trust in democracy and a mistrust of bureaucracy;
- an interest in reaching out to diverse cultural communities that is rooted in the country's diverse cultural origins;
- a lack of trust in external intervention but confidence in "a little help" locally when it is needed;
- a distrust of heavy-handed supervision and testing.

Lest this optimism about ourselves appear unbridled, we state again that the current period is one of latency for authentic reform. The language of reform in education is still dominated by the harshness of individuality, incrementalism, control, bureaucracy, competition, and intervention. It is a discouraging language of distrust that gives up on the viability of the future of millions of children. It is inherently racist and sexist. We have not, as yet, found a way to introduce a more effective language of possibility, but we must do so.

As a beginning, we could shuck off the assumptions that have led us to adopt the current reform agenda. That is not an impossible task. If we examine the dominant assumptions one-by-one, their efficacy is easily doubted. We also need to place certain priorities at the top of our agenda. They are not radical priorities. They emphasize saving our children and youth through a people-sensitive reform movement. Will such a movement have trade-offs? Of course. Every policy choice has trade-offs. But in this case they seem modest when weighed against the agony of failure and neglect that currently confronts American children.

Will a school reform movement that is child-centered and brooks no talk of failure in caring for our children cost money? Of course it will, but it is no more than parents are willing to invest in their own children.

Do we need a long period of experimentation to support the reform? No, we already know enough to revolutionize the education of our youth. We are not failing because we lack technical expertise. If that were so, individual classrooms and schools would all share the failure. We need to make ordinary what is now exceptional; and that will require adopting a new purpose, not a new test or a new curriculum. Once this new purpose is established, the costs of trade-offs can be lessened, in some cases by attending to multiple policy positions. The metaphor for tomorrow's school should be the successful home, guided by mature and caring adults:

- supporting success hopefully and endlessly;
- adjusting to the phases of childhood and young adulthood with trust, confidence, support, and challenge;
- being there all the time, being open when danger and failure threatens;
- believing in the efficacy of the individual during periods of failure as well as success;
- providing the basic conditions for nurturance, protection, and growth, including social, medical, nutritional, and psychological assistance when they are needed;
- fostering collegiality, cooperation, and collaboration as teachers and students learn and play together;
- introducing the wonder of a diverse and ever-changing world to the learner;
- taking time every day for the personal, interactive relationships needed to support learning;
- assessing success and failure — building on the former, learning from the latter.

No one can reform our schools for us. If there is to be authentic reform in American education, it will result from a grassroots movement. Systemic reformers will have to be resisted systematically. They are distracting us from the job at hand. The only system we have is the local school; and external agencies should be worrying about how they can help and support these school units, not how they can dominate them. Current repressive and retrogressive policies will have to be rejected and replaced by hopeful, teacher- and student-centered reforms. We are honestly sorry that those who would save our children and our schools by fiat cannot do it. But we will have to do it in individual communities through hard work, individual investment and effort, and local reformers who work on the line. Isn't that always the way?

REFERENCES

Adelman, C. "Turn Diplomas into Report Cards." *New York Times*, 19 June 1993, p. 21.

American Association of University Women. *How Schools Shortchange Girls*. Washington, D.C: AAUW Educational Foundation, National Education Association, 1992.

Angus, L. " 'New' Leadership and the Possibility of Education Reform." *In Critical Perspectives on Educational Leadership*, edited by J. Smyth. Philadelphia: Falmer Press, 1989.

Argyris, C. *Personality and Organization: The Conflict Between System and the Individual*. New York: Harper and Brothers, 1957.

Aronowitz, S., and Giroux, H.A. *Education Still Under Siege*. New York: Bergin & Garvey, 1994.

Barnard, C. *The Functions of the Executive*. Cambridge, Mass.: Harvard University, 1938.

Berliner, D.C. "Education Reform in an Era of Disinformation." Paper presented at the meeting of the American Association of Colleges for Teacher Education, San Antonio, Texas, 1992.

Burrell, G., and Morgan, G. *Sociological Paradigms and Organizational Analysis*. London: Heinemann, 1979.

Clark, D.L. "In Consideration of Goal-Free Planning: The Failure of Traditional Planning Systems in Education." *Educational Administration Quarterly* 17, no. 3 (1981): 42-60.

Clark, D.L., and Astuto, T.A. "Paradoxical Choice Options in Organizations." In *Leaders for America's Schools: The Report and Papers of the National Commission on Excellence in Educational Administration*, edited by D.E. Griffiths, R.T. Stout, and P.B. Forsyth. Berkeley, Calif.: McCutchan, 1988.

Clark, D.L., and Astuto, T.A. "An Assessment of Changes in Federal Educational Policy During the Reagan Administration." *In Policy Issues for the 90s: Policy Studies Review Annual*, vol. 9, edited by R.C. Rist. New Brunswick, N.J.: Transaction, 1989. a

Clark, D.L., and Astuto, T.A. "The Disjunction of Federal Educational Policy and National Educational Needs in the 1990s." In *Education Politics for the New Century: The Twentieth Anniversary Yearbook of the Politics of Education Association*, edited by D.E. Mitchell and M.E. Goertz. London: Falmer, 1989. b

Coder, J.; Rainwater, L.; and Smeeding, T. "Inequality in Ten Modern Nations: The United States in an International Context." *American Economic Review* 79, no. 2 (1989): 320-24.

Cohen, J. "Constructing Race at an Urban High School: In Their Minds, Their Mouths, Their Hearts." In *Beyond Silenced Voices: Class, Race, and Gender in United States Schools*, edited by L. Weis and M. Fine. Albany: State University of New York Press, 1993.

Coleman, J.S.; Campbell, E.Q.; Hobson, C.J.; McPartland, J.; Mood, A.M.; Weinfeld, F.E.; and York, R.L. *Equality of Educational Opportunity.* Washington, D.C.: U.S. Government Printing Office, 1966.

Cummins, J. "Empowering Minority Students: A Framework for Intervention." In *Beyond Silenced Voices: Class, Race, and Gender in United States Schools,* edited by L. Weis and M. Fine. Albany: State University of New York Press, 1993.

Delpit, L.D. "The Silenced Dialogue: Power and Pedagogy in Educating Other People's Children." In *Beyond Silenced Voices: Class, Race, and Gender in United States Schools,* edited by L. Weis and M. Fine. Albany: State University of New York Press, 1993.

Doyle, W. "Curriculum and Pedagogy." In *Handbook of Research on Curriculum,* edited by P.W. Jackson. New York: Macmillan, 1992.

Edmonds, R. "Effective Schools for the Urban Poor." *Educational Leadership* 37, no. 1 (1979): 15-18, 20-24.

Elmore, R.F. *Restructuring Schools.* San Francisco: Jossey-Bass, 1990.

Epstein, J. "The Forum." *Teachers College Record* 94, no. 4 (1993): 710-17.

Fine, M. "Why Urban Adolescents Drop Into and Out of Public High School." In *School Dropouts: Patterns and Policies,* edited by G. Natriello. New York: Teachers College Press, 1987.

Fine, M. *Framing Dropouts: Notes on the Politics of an Urban Public High School.* Albany: State University of New York Press, 1991.

Fine, M. "[A]parent Involvement: Reflections on Parents, Power, and Urban Public Schools." *Teachers College Record* 94, no. 4 (1993): 682-710. a

Fine, M. "Sexuality, Schooling, and Adolescent Females: The Missing Discourse of Desire." In *Beyond Silenced Voices: Class, Race, and Gender in United States Schools,* edited by L. Weis and M. Fine. Albany: State University of New York Press, 1993. b

Friedenberg, E.Z. "Images of Education Reform." *The Review of Education* 14, no. 1 (1991): 9-16.

Fullan, M.G. *The New Meaning of Educational Change.* New York: Teachers College Press, 1991.

Gillespie, D.F., and Mileti, D.S. *Technostructures and Interorganizational Relations.* Lexington, Mass.: Lexington Books, 1979.

Giroux, H. "Rewriting the Politics of Identity and Difference." *The Review of Education* 14, no. 4 (1992): 305-15.

Grannis, J.; Riehl, C.; Pallas, A.M.; Lerer, N.; Randolph, S.; and Jewell, K. *Evaluation of the New York City Dropout Prevention Initiative: Final Report on the High Schools for Year Two, 1986-1987.* New York: Institute for Urban and Minority Education, Teachers College, Columbia University, 1988.

Hamburg, D.A. *Today's Children: Creating a Future for a Generation in Crisis.* New York: Times Books, 1992.

Haney, W. "Testing and Minorities." In *Beyond Silenced Voices: Class, Race, and Gender in United States Schools,* edited by L. Weis and M. Fine. Albany: State University of New York Press, 1993.

Herzberg, F. *The Managerial Choice: To Be Efficient and to Be Human*. Homewood, Ill.: Dow Jones-Irwin, 1976.

Hewlett, S.A. *When the Bough Breaks: The Cost of Neglecting Our Children*. New York: Basic Books, 1991.

Hodgkinson, H.L. *The Same Client: The Demographics of Education and Service Delivery Systems*. Washington, D.C.: Institute for Educational Leadership, 1989.

Huelskamp, R.M. "Perspectives on Education in America." *Phi Delta Kappan* 74 (May 1993): 718-21.

Jackson, P.W. "Conceptions of Curriculum and Curriculum Specialists." In *Handbook of Research on Curriculum*, edited by P.W. Jackson. New York: Macmillan, 1992.

Johnson, S.M. *Teachers at Work: Achieving Success in Our Schools*. New York: Basic Books, 1990.

Kozol, J. "Corporate Raid on Education: Whittle and the Privateers." *The Nation* 255, no. 8 (1992): 272-78.

Lawler, E. *Pay and Organization Development*. Reading, Mass.: Addison-Wesley, 1981.

Lightfoot, S.L. "The Lives of Teachers." In *Handbook of Teaching and Policy*, edited by L.S. Shulman and G. Sykes. New York: Longman, 1983.

Little, J.W. "Norms of Collegiality and Experimentation: Workplace Conditions of School Success." *American Educational Research Journal* 19, no. 3 (1982): 325-40.

Little, J.W. "Conditions of Professional Development in Secondary Schools." In *The Contexts of Teaching in Secondary Schools: Teachers' Realities*, edited by M.W. McLaughlin, J.E. Talbert, and N. Bascia. New York: Teachers College Press, 1990.

Maslow, A.H. "A Theory of Human Motivation." 1943. Reprinted in *Classics of Public Administration*, edited by J.M. Shafritz and A.C. Hyde. Pacific Grove, Calif.: Brooks/Cole, 1987.

McGregor, D. *The Human Side of Enterprise*. New York: McGraw-Hill, 1960.

Meier, D.W. "Get the Story Straight: Myths, Lies, and Public Schools." *The Nation* 255, no. 8 (1992): 271-72.

National Commission on Excellence in Education. *A Nation at Risk: The Imperative for Educational Reform*. Washington, D.C.: U.S. Government Printing Office, 1983.

Natriello, G.; McDill, E.L.; and Pallas, A.M. *Schooling Disadvantaged Children: Racing Against Catastrophe*. New York: Teachers College Press, 1990.

Oakes, J.; Gamoran, A.; and Page, R.N. "Curriculum Differentiation: Opportunities, Outcomes, and Meanings." In *Handbook of Research on Curriculum*, edited by P.W. Jackson. New York: Macmillan, 1992.

Ogbu, J. "Understanding Cultural Diversity and Learning." *Educational Researcher* 21, no. 8 (1992): 5-13.

Percy, W. *The Thanatos Syndrome*. New York: Farrar, Straus, Giroux, 1987.

Peters, T., and Waterman, R., Jr. *In Search of Excellence: Lessons from America's Best-Run Companies*. New York: Harper & Row, 1982.

Polakow, V. "Invisible Voices and Visible Spaces: Do Young Children Matter Existentially?" *The Review of Education* 14, no. 4 (1992): 295-303.

101

Reagan, T. "More of the Same: Reforms of American Public Schooling and the Minority Language Student." In *The New Servants of Power: A Critique of the 1980s School Reform Movement,* edited by C. Shea, E. Kahane, and P. Sola. Westport, Conn.: Praeger, 1989.

Rosenshine, B., and Stevens, R. "Teaching Functions." In *Handbook of Research on Teaching,* 3rd ed., edited by M.C. Wittrock. New York: Macmillan, 1986.

Sarason, S.B. *The Predictable Failure of Education Reform.* San Francisco: Jossey-Bass, 1990.

Shea, C. "Pentagon vs. Multinational Capitalism: The Political Economy of the 1980's School Reform Movement." In *The New Servants of Power: A Critique of the 1980s School Reform Movement,* edited by C. Shea, E. Kahane, and P. Sola. Westport, Conn.: Praeger, 1989.

Sizer, T. *Horace's Compromise: The Dilemma of the American High School.* Boston: Houghton-Mifflin, 1984.

Taylor, F.W. "The Principles of Scientific Management." 1916. Reprinted in *Classics of Organization Theory,* 2nd ed., edited by J.M. Shafritz and J.S. Ott. Chicago: Dorsey, 1987.

Weick, K.E. *The Social Psychology of Organizing.* Reading, Mass.; Addison-Wesley, 1979.

Westbury, I. "Comparing American and Japanese Achievement: Is the United States Really a Low Achiever?" *Educational Researcher* 21, no. 5 (1992): 18-24.

Willensky, J. "The Politics of the Postmodern." *The Review of Education* 14, no. 4 (1992): 343-51.

William T. Grant Foundation Commission on Work, Family and Citizenship. *The Forgotten Half: Pathways to Success for America's Youth and Young Families.* Washington, D.C., 1988.

Wittrock, M.C. "Students' Thought Processes." In *Handbook of Research on Teaching,* 3rd ed., edited by M.C. Wittrock. New York: Macmillan, 1986.

ABOUT THE AUTHORS

Terry A. Astuto is a professor of educational administration and director of the Program in Educational Administration and Supervision at New York University. Her research and writing have explored the application to education of alternative perspectives in organizational theory and contemporary issues in education policy.

David L. Clark is Kenan Professor of Education in the Program in Educational Leadership at the University of North Carolina at Chapel Hill. His research and writing have dealt with issues in federal policy in education and organizational theory. Recently his focus has turned to current efforts to reform American education.

Anne-Marie Read is a doctoral candidate in the Program in Educational Leadership, School of Education, University of North Carolina at Chapel Hill. She currently is investigating the reactions of doctoral students to advanced graduate study based on alternative ways of viewing schools and school reform.

Kathleen McGree is a doctoral candidate in the Program in Educational Studies, Curry School of Education, University of Virginia. She currently is investigating the ways in which secondary students experience school and how they view contemporary education reform initiatives.

L. deKoven Pelton Fernandez is a doctoral candidate in the Program in Educational Leadership and Policy Studies, Curry School of Education, University of Virginia. Her research is about the school experiences of girls and the implications of a feminist critique for school restructuring.